W9-CDW-253

AMERICAN HERITAGE
ILLUSTRATED HISTORY
OF THE UNITED STATES

FREE LIBRARY OF PHILADELPHIA

A Civil War version of the U.S.O. provided in one building (top picture) a place for soldiers to shave (left), eat (center), and wash clothes (right).

FRONT COVER: *Union and Confederate infantry are seen in close combat in this Currier and Ives lithograph of the Second Battle of Bull Run, fought at Manassas, Virginia on April 29, 1862.*
LIBRARY OF CONGRESS

FRONT ENDSHEET: *A militia regiment from New York, dressed in blue coats and red trousers, prepares for inspection in an 1861 painting by James Walker.*
ALEXANDER MCCOOK CRAIGHEAD COLLECTION

CONTENTS PAGE: *This painted panel is one of the four from Lincoln's private railroad car. One of the others shows a Washington portrait; two are landscapes.*
JOSLYN ART MUSEUM

BACK ENDSHEET: *Some of Lee's soldiers fold their flag for the final time. Many Southern regiments burned their flags rather than surrender them.*
ALEXANDER MCCOOK CRAIGHEAD COLLECTION

BACK COVER: *President Abraham Lincoln (top right) was painted by G.P.A. Healy; Frederick Douglass (top left) a former slave, was a leading abolitionist journalist; the Confederate "Stars and Bars" flag is furled for the last time when General Lee surrendered in 1865.*
THE CORCORAN GALLERY OF ART MUSEUM PURCHASE, GALLERY FUND 1879; LIBRARY OF CONGRESS; WEST POINT MUSEUM COLLECTIONS, U.S. MILITARY COLLECTIONS

AMERICAN HERITAGE
ILLUSTRATED HISTORY
OF THE UNITED STATES

VOLUME 8

THE CIVIL WAR

BY ROBERT G. ATHEARN

Created in Association with the
Editors of AMERICAN HERITAGE

and for the updated edition
MEDIA PROJECTS INCORPORATED

CHOICE PUBLISHING, INC.
New York

© 1988, 1971, 1967, 1963 by American Heritage, a division of Forbes Inc. All rights reserved. No part of this work may be reproduced or transmitted in any form or by any means, electronic or mechanical, including photocopying and recording, or by any information storage or retrieval system without permission in writing from the publisher.

Library of Congress Catalog Card Number: 87-73399
ISBN 0-945260-08-3

This 1988 edition is published and distributed by Choice Publishing, Inc., 53 Watermill Lane, Great Neck, NY 11021 by arrangement with American Heritage, a division of Forbes, Inc.

Manufactured in the United States of America

CONTENTS OF THE COMPLETE SERIES

Editor's Note to the Revised Edition
Introduction by ALLAN NEVINS
Main text by ROBERT G. ATHEARN

EACH VOLUME CONTAINS AN ENCYCLOPEDIC SECTION; MASTER INDEX IN VOLUME 18

CONTENTS OF VOLUME 8

CHAPTER 22

THE WAR COMES

The Confederate bombardment of Fort Sumter sparked a great military conflagration that was to blaze in America for four bitter, bloody years.

In the days following Sumter's surrender, President Abraham Lincoln called for 75,000 volunteers, declared a naval blockade of Southern ports, and ordered a special session of Congress. These events electrified the North and sent thousands of young men scurrying to the recruiting offices. Reaction in the South was much the same. Virginia, Arkansas, North Carolina, and Tennessee soon joined the seven states that had formed the Confederate States of America. Southerners answered the call to the colors as enthusiastically as Northerners.

Neither side expected a long war. Northern boys were called up for 90 days—plenty of time, it was thought, to crush the "insurrection." Southerners were equally optimistic, anticipating a quick march on Washington to dispose of Lincoln and the "Black

N. S. MEYER

The drummer boy, youngest of the soldiers on both sides in the Civil War, seems forlorn and lost as he stands in a barren camp in this Julian Scott painting.

Republicans." Both armies were little more than collections of state militia, thrown together with the idea of delivering one hammer blow and then returning home for the fall harvest.

As harried officers tried to whip some semblance of order and discipline into these raw levies, Lincoln turned his attention to the crucial and wavering border states of Maryland, Missouri, and Kentucky. Rioting broke out in Baltimore and St. Louis, with Union troops and civilians fighting in the streets, but vigorous and hard-handed action by the federal government kept both Maryland and Missouri from seceding. Confederate President Jefferson Davis and Lincoln played a cat-and-mouse game with Kentucky, each hoping the other would shatter the state's precarious neutrality. Eventually Northern troops got the upper hand, and Kentucky, too, remained in the Union.

The nation's attention quickly focused on Washington and Richmond, the two capitals, just 100 miles apart. Members of Congress pressed the army to advance on Richmond. Army officers were anxious also, for the 90-day enlistment period was drawing to

The 6th Massachusetts Regiment was on its way to Washington on April 19, 1861, traveling through Baltimore, when it was attacked by Southern sympathizers.

a close. Old Winfield Scott, whose army service dated back to the War of 1812, was in charge of the military preparations. He appointed Brigadier General Irvin McDowell to lead the assault on the Confederate force at Manassas, 25 miles southwest of Washington. McDowell protested to the President that his troops were far from ready for a fight. "You are green, it is true," Lincoln replied, "but they are green also. You are all green alike."

On July 21, 1861, the two armies clashed near a little stream called Bull Run. McDowell's thrust was at first successful. Then his attack fell apart in the face of stiffening resistance, and the Federals withdrew toward Washington. The retreat became a rout, but the Southern troops were too disorganized to follow up their victory.

Bull Run threw the North into a state of shock. It was hard to believe that Union troops had met with such a reverse. Angered and determined, the North began to reorganize its forces. McDowell was replaced by young, self-confident Major General George B. McClellan, who already had won a series of small victories in

COLLECTION OF ALEXANDER McCOOK CRAIGHEAD

western Virginia. When General Scott retired in November, McClellan replaced him as general-in-chief of the Union Army. McClellan was a first-rate organizer and drillmaster, and during the winter his Army of the Potomac began to assume the look of a real fighting force. There were many in the North who still felt one more battle would put an end to the rebellion.

Real war begins

The new year of 1862 began auspiciously for the Union. A series of victories in the Western theater demolished the Confederate defense line that ran from Cumberland Gap in the Alleghenies to the Mississippi River. On January 19, Brigadier General George Thomas won a fight at Mill Springs to wrest eastern Kentucky from the Confederates. On February 6, an obscure brigadier general named Ulysses S. Grant, cooperating with a fleet of gunboats under Flag Officer Andrew Foote, captured Fort Henry on the Tennessee River.

Within a week, Grant had laid siege to Fort Donelson, 12 miles away on the Cumberland River. When the Con-

Jefferson Davis is in the center of this anonymous painting, with four of the Southern military leaders—Beauregard, Jackson, Stuart, and Johnston.

federate commander requested surrender terms, Grant replied bluntly, "No terms except an immediate and unconditional surrender can be accepted." Fort Donelson and its 15,000 defenders gave up on February 16, and the entire center of the Confederate defense line was gone. At once the taciturn man from Illinois became known as Unconditional Surrender Grant, and the North had a new hero.

The Richmond government desperately rallied its forces to try to regain the initiative in the Mississippi Valley, an area it could not afford to lose. General Albert Sidney Johnston assembled a striking force at Corinth, Mississippi, just below the Tennessee border, and looked for a chance to launch a counterattack.

He soon found it. Grant had advanced up the Tennessee River as far as Pittsburg Landing, where he encamped his army near a little country meetinghouse called Shiloh Church to await reinforcements. At dawn on April 6, Johnston struck hard at the unwary Federals. By nightfall the Confederates had pushed Grant's army almost into the river. But the Federals received reinforcements, and the next day Grant's counterattack drove the enemy back to Corinth.

The Battle of Shiloh was fought by soldiers largely untrained but fiercely determined, and the casualty lists—more than a third of the 77,000 men engaged were shot, with General Johnston among the dead—stunned both North and South. Hopes for a quick and comparatively bloodless end to the war died among the peach blossoms at Shiloh.

Federal forces in the West kept up the relentless pressure. The Mississippi River stronghold of Island Num-

M. AND M. KAROLIK COLLECTION, MUSEUM OF FINE ARTS, BOSTON

ber 10 fell to Union troops, and a brief, savage naval battle featuring ironclad gunboats opened the river as far south as Memphis, Tennessee. As the Confederates apprehensively looked northward, Flag Officer David G. Farragut's powerful squadron battered its way past the forts guarding New Orleans and on April 25 gobbled up the largest city in the Confederacy. The South's hold on the great river was soon reduced to the 250 miles between the citadels of Port Hudson, Louisiana, and Vicksburg, Mississippi.

While these important victories were being won in the West, McClellan (whom the newspapers had nicknamed the Young Napoleon) was having his troubles in the East. Pressure was exerted upon him from every side to advance on Richmond. He had no capacity for understanding the political aspects of a civil war, and he soon had

NATIONAL ARCHIVES

George B. McClellan

McClellan was in charge of the unsuccessful advance on Richmond made in 1862. He is shown below riding at the head of his staff, surveying the camp set up for the campaign on the Pamunkey River in Virginia.

CHICAGO HISTORICAL SOCIETY

Entered according to Act of Congress
in the Year 1885 by the
McCORMICK HARVESTING MACHINE CO.
in the Office of the
Librarian of Congress at Washington.

·BATTLE OF SHI

THE "McCORMICK" MACHINES COME VICT

PRESENTED WITH COMPLIMENTS (

This print of the Battle of Shiloh is of the area where the fighting was so fierce that it was

·APRIL 6ᵀᴴ 1862·

F EVERY CONTEST, AND WITHOUT A SCRATCH.

RVESTING MACHINE COMPANY

COPIED BY SPECIAL PERMISSION
From The
·PANORAMA PAINTING·
ON EXHIBITION IN CHICAGO

I. General Grant and Staff

later referred to as the Hornet's Nest. Grant and his staff are on the mound at the right.

much of official Washington on his neck. In March, 1862, he was goaded into action.

McClellan rejected the direct overland route to Richmond; instead, he ferried his army down Chesapeake Bay and landed it at the tip of the Virginia Peninsula. His idea was to advance the 70 miles to Richmond with Union naval forces on the York and James Rivers protecting both flanks. To appease President Lincoln, he left 40,000 troops to protect Washington—troops he expected to join him when he laid siege to Richmond.

Lee takes a command

It took the cautious general two months to get within sight of the Confederate capital. The rebels under General Joseph E. Johnston fell back until May 31, when Johnston counterattacked at Fair Oaks. The two-day battle was indecisive, but one result was to have a far-reaching effect on the Civil War. Johnston was seriously wounded, and President Davis appointed General Robert E. Lee to command in his place.

Lee had been generally considered the best officer in the United States Army, and General Scott had offered him command of the main federal forces after Fort Sumter. It was an agonizing decision, but the Virginian chose to follow his state out of the Union. He served as Davis' military adviser until the Confederate President put him in command of the Army of Northern Virginia. Lee led it until

T.S.C. Lowe's federal observation balloon was used to study the rebel battlefields.

he surrendered at Appomattox.

Even before he took command, Lee had conceived a strategy to prevent the federal reinforcements in the Washington area from descending on Richmond from the north as McClellan advanced from the east. The instrument of that strategy was General Thomas Jackson, a former professor at the Virginia Military Institute who had won his nickname of Stonewall at Bull Run and who was proving to have a positive taste for war.

Jackson's small force slipped into the Shenandoah Valley and began to upset the Washington government.

LIBRARY OF CONGRESS

Federal units (including McClellan's reinforcements) descended on Jackson from all sides. His answer was one of the dazzling campaigns of the war. "All Old Jackson gave us was a musket, a hundred rounds, and a gum blanket, and he druv us like hell," one of his men said. Within a month he won five battles, tied up more than 50,000 Union troops, and then slipped away to join Lee at Richmond.

Lee now took the offensive. In the Seven Days' Battles he repeatedly attacked McClellan's force and drove it all the way across the Virginia Peninsula to the James River. Lee could never quite bring the Federals to a decision, but McClellan was a beaten

McClellan's vast train—4,300 wagons and ambulances—fords Bear Creek near Savage's Station on the harassed retreat of the Union forces from Richmond.

man, his only thought being to save his army.

McClellan blamed his defeat on the politicians in Washington, but Lincoln chose not to debate with his general over what might have been. Instead, he turned to the Western theater and brought to Washington two generals who, he hoped, would get the war back on the right track. To replace McClellan as general-in-chief, he installed a fussy, bookish soldier named Henry Halleck, known irreverently in the regular army as Old Brains. To command a new field army composed of the troops around Washington and the parts of McClellan's force being evacuated from the peninsula, the President chose pompous, opinionated John Pope. (Pope seems to have been one of the few men Robert E. Lee actively despised. Pope, Lee ordered, was to be "suppressed.")

Lee hastened to strike before McClellan's troops could be firmly joined with Pope's. Stonewall Jackson slipped around Pope's flank with half of the Confederate Army and led the Union general a chase until he let himself be brought to bay on the old Bull Run battlefield. Meanwhile, the other wing of Lee's army, under James Longstreet, was stealthily approaching. Jackson beat off Pope's determined attacks on August 29, but when Pope renewed the assault the next day, Longstreet sprang the trap and sent the Federals into headlong flight. John Pope had indeed been suppressed. He was sent off to fight Indians and McClellan got his army back.

The Second Battle of Bull Run left angry disgust in the minds of the hard-war wing of the Republican Party, a clique known as the Radicals. They needed a scapegoat, so they descended on General Fitz-John Porter, whom Pope accused of disobeying a battlefield order. (The order had been impossible to obey; Porter was aware of Longstreet's presence even if Pope was not. But that made no difference

Dejected Yankee soldiers survey a row of boxcars burned to their trucks by Stonewall Jackson in his raid on Pope's supply base at Manassas Junction.

to the Radicals.) Senator Zachariah Chandler of Michigan wondered why Pope had ever let Porter leave the battlefield alive after such cowardice in the face of the enemy. Senator Benjamin "Bluff Ben" Wade of Ohio was already on record as saying that generals should never even consider retreat, adding that if the soldiers could not win a victory, they ought to come home in their coffins.

As a result of all this, Porter, a good fighting general with the wrong political connections, was railroaded out of the army. Wade's notorious Joint Committee on the Conduct of the War gained new strength. It would plague President Lincoln until the war was over, and strike fear into the hearts of his generals.

Southern high tide

Lee determined to keep the initiative, and he launched an invasion of the North. McClellan wrote his wife, "Again I have been called upon to save the country," and set out in cautious pursuit. At the same time, in the Western theater, Braxton Bragg's Confederate Army of Tennessee drove headlong into Kentucky, thrusting for the Ohio River. For the only time in the Civil War, the South was making a coordinated effort to invade and subdue the North. The fall of 1862 was to mark the high tide of the Confederacy.

With James E. B. "Jeb" Stuart's cavalry screening his advance from the Yankees, Lee slipped into the Shenan-

Stonewall Jackson

COOK COLLECTION, VALENTINE MUSEUM

LIBRARY OF CONGRESS

doah Valley. Half the Confederate Army was detached to seize the Union garrison at Harpers Ferry, astride Lee's line of communications. But now fate stepped in to give McClellan a helping hand: An Indiana corporal stumbled on a lost copy of Lee's orders that had been wrapped around three cigars. McClellan realized he was closer to the parts of Lee's army than they were to each other. But he did not move quite fast enough. Lee pulled together his scattered forces in a precarious position on the banks of Antietam Creek near the hamlet of Sharpsburg, Maryland.

McClellan was a superb military housekeeper, and the men of the Army of the Potomac loved him as they loved no other of their numerous commanders. But in the heat of battle

Burnside, by taking more than three hours to cross a bridge over an easily forded stream, seriously delayed the Union thrust at the Battle of Antietam.

something went out of him. On September 17, the Federals repeatedly attacked Lee's lines, and by the narrowest of margins repeatedly failed to break through. "The sun seemed almost to go backwards," a rebel soldier wrote. "It appeared as if night would never come."

Antietam was a bitterly fought battle, and it cost more men killed and wounded—some 23,500—than any other single day in the Civil War. McClellan could not nerve himself to throw in his reserves for one final blow, and the battle was a standoff. Lee aggressively held his battered army in its lines for another day, then retreated across the Potomac River into Virginia. One wing of the Confederate invasion had failed.

In the West, however, the Union had a crisis to face, and it was the legacy of Old Brains Halleck. After Grant's victory at Shiloh, Halleck stepped in to gather up the fruits. But he made war by the book. He scattered his immense forces far and wide, garrisoning captured territory and rebuilding railroads, and the Confederates were given time to recuperate. Braxton Bragg neatly slipped the leash Union General Don Carlos Buell was holding and headed for the Northern heartland. Bragg was nearly to Louisville before he turned off to install a secessionist government in the Kentucky capital of Frankfort. As a result, Buell got between the Southerners and the Ohio River.

The two armies finally stumbled into each other near the town of Perryville, Kentucky, on October 8. It was a strange battle, with neither commander apparently aware of what was going on. Like Antietam, Perryville was indecisive; and like McClellan, Bragg seemed to lose his grip in the test of combat. He gathered up his forces and tramped back to Tennessee.

Although Antietam and Perryville were not military victories for the Union, they did stop the South's drive into the North and cut Southern hopes for foreign intervention, based upon its successful campaigns. Also, after Lincoln announced the Emancipation Proclamation, broadening the conflict into a struggle to free the slaves, the possibility of foreign support was further hindered.

To Europe, and particularly to England, the outbreak of war in the United States had seemed to spell opportunity. For years some Britons had watched with anxiety as America grew in commercial and industrial importance, and as the major users of Southern cotton, they resented the high tariff walls that kept them from trading their manufactures for it. If the aristocratic classes of Great Britain and France had their way, the Confederacy might have received direct military aid.

Southern agents worked long and hard to bring this about. After the Emancipation Proclamation, however, Britain's middle classes and workers, with all liberals and humanitarians, clearly saw the Civil War as a struggle to end slavery. A civilized power could hardly go to war for a cause that endorsed human bondage, or actively support it. The South's dream of foreign intervention now guttered out like a candle in a windstorm.

Stalemate

Two weeks after Antietam, McClellan was still in Maryland, suffering from what Lincoln described as "the slows." While the Union commander temporized, Jeb Stuart's troopers rode completely around his army on a reconnaissance. This was the sort of exploit that the hard-fighting, flamboyant Stuart loved (he had done it before, on the Virginia Peninsula), and understandably the people of the North were furious. Lincoln's patience was exhausted, and he made a clean sweep: McClellan was out and Major General Ambrose Burnside was in as commander of the Army of the Potomac; in the West, William S. Rosecrans replaced Buell—he, too, had the slows—as head of the Union Army of the Tennessee.

Burnside honestly protested that he was not up to the job, but he dutifully moved southward to the Rappahannock River opposite Fredericksburg. There he sat waiting for the belated arrival of his pontoon bridges while Lee efficiently fortified the heights behind the town. At last Burnside crossed

COLLECTION OF WALTER LORD

the river, and on December 13, 1862, launched a massive frontal attack on the rebel lines.

Up the incline moved waves of blue-clad soldiers, stubbornly facing the flaming Confederate guns and being slaughtered like cattle. As the attackers slipped in the blood of their comrades and stumbled over fallen bodies, the rebels watched in awe. George Pickett, to find immortality the following year at Gettysburg, wrote his wife that the "brilliant assault . . . was beyond description. Why, my darling, we forgot they were fighting us, and cheer after cheer went up all along our lines."

It was a brutal, senseless kind of bravery—that of men following their orders in an ill-conceived attack upon a well-entrenched enemy. Burnside lost 13,000 men, Lee fewer than 5,000. When the awful facts of this debacle came home to the people in the North, confidence in the Lincoln administration waned and attacks on the President reached new heights. Senator Wade's Joint Committee on the Conduct of the War rose to new paroxysms of fury, for it had hoped to establish Burnside as its latest hero. On January 25, 1863, Lincoln removed Burnside and replaced him with Major General Joseph Hooker. He was the Army of the Potomac's fifth commander in a year and a half of fighting.

In Tennessee, Rosecrans began a drive to capture Chattanooga, gate-

CULVER PICTURES

COLLECTION OF ALEXANDER McCOOK CRAIGHEAD

After the defeat at Fredericksburg, Burnside and his men went up the Rappahannock under such foul conditions that the move was called the Mud March.

The Mississippi made a loop at Vicksburg, and Grant set his men to digging canals in an attempt to divert the river and so bypass the city's defenses.

way to the Deep South. At Murfreesboro he found his way blocked by Bragg. On December 31, both commanders planned to hold with their right wing and attack with their left; had they carried this out, the two armies might have turned around each other as if caught in a gigantic revolving door. But Bragg struck first and bent the Union force back on itself. Rosecrans rallied, and on January 2, 1863, won back his lost ground. Each army lost about a quarter of its strength; neither was in condition to resume the contest for six full months.

Two new generals and two new battles, and the Union was no closer to victory. The ever-growing casualty lists seemed to testify that the Northern cause was stalled on dead center. And along the Mississippi River, as the weeks of the new year passed, it appeared that Unconditional Sur-

render Grant, too, had struck a stone wall trying to subdue Vicksburg.

The turning point

The great Confederate fortress was perched on a bluff overlooking a bend in the Mississippi, impregnable to attack from the river. The swampy character of the terrain made it hard for Grant even to find dry ground from which to launch an attack on the land side. Through the winter of 1862–63, he and his lieutenant—red-haired, volatile William Tecumseh Sherman —tried and rejected one scheme after another to get at the citadel. The Federals dug canals and cut levees and made channels through bayous, and at one point nearly lost Rear Admiral David Dixon Porter's gunboat squadron in a watery maze.

In April, 1863, Grant finally perfected a daring plan. He marched his

649

COLLECTION OF ALEXANDER McCOOK CRAIGHEAD

army down the Louisiana side of the river opposite Vicksburg. Porter sped his fleet of gunboats and transports past the thundering Vicksburg batteries on the night of April 16 and ferried Grant's force across the river below the city. If Grant's campaign failed, the vessels would be stuck there, for they were too under-powered to beat their way upstream again past the batteries.

To solve the supply problem, the Union soldiers were ordered to live off the country, although they were outnumbered and deep in enemy territory. Grant proposed to isolate the Vicksburg garrison before it could be reinforced by Confederate units

650

from central Mississippi. In a whirl-wind campaign reminiscent of Stone-wall Jackson's effort in the Shenan-doah Valley the previous year, he won five battles in less than three weeks, severed Vicksburg's lifelines, and besieged the city.

In Virginia meanwhile, Hooker was moving against Lee's Army of North-

James Walker's painting records the charge of A.P. Hill's rebels on the first day at Gettysburg. Hill's men have overrun the Union line on McPherson's Ridge. Eventually the federal troops were out-flanked and driven back to a last-stand position around the seminary building in the middle distance. At the left, in the distance, are Culp's and Cemetery Hills, and at the right, the Round Tops—all important Union posts on the next days.

NEW HAMPSHIRE HISTORICAL SOCIETY

LIBRARY OF CONGRESS

ern Virginia. He said he hoped God would have mercy on General Lee, "for I will have none." But Lee liked to pick his own places to fight, and he chose a tangled woodland along the Rappahannock River west of Fredericksburg known as the Wilderness. Hooker had not intended to fight there, and his grand plans began to evaporate in the clouds of battle smoke that enveloped the crossroads hamlet of Chancellorsville.

Outnumbered two to one, Lee gambled once more—and won. He gave Jackson half his force and sent him off on a long flanking march. In the late afternoon of May 2, Jackson struck the Union right flank and crushed it. In four more days of heavy

George Gordon Meade

Nearly the entire battlefield at Gettysburg is shown in James Walker's painting of the final day. General Meade is visible just right of center, mounted, with field glass. Below, the Union forces, in the rain, pursue Lee's army.

LIBRARY OF CONGRESS

653

fighting, Lee pinned the Army of the Potomac against the Rappahannock. When he turned and routed a relieving force, the whole Union army pulled back across the river. Chancellorsville was Lee's most brilliant victory, but it was a costly one. Stonewall Jackson was mortally wounded, shot accidentally by his own men. Lee mourned, "I have lost my right arm."

In the frantic hope of forcing Grant to give up his siege of Vicksburg and bring his army east, Lee now initiated a gigantic raid against the North. He divided his veteran army into three corps, under James Longstreet, Richard Ewell, and A. P. Hill, and raced through the Shenandoah Valley and into Pennsylvania. Hooker shadowed him skillfully, but he had clearly lost the confidence of President Lincoln. On June 28, Major General George Gordon Meade, a capable and irascible veteran, took command of the Army of the Potomac. Just four days later, on July 1, advance elements of both armies collided at the Pennsylvania market town of Gettysburg. The greatest battle of the Civil War had begun.

The first day of Gettysburg was a decided victory for Lee, who was able to pour more men into the widening battle than Meade. The Federals were driven through the town to a fishhook-shaped area of high ground. Its shank was known as Cemetery Ridge. On July 2, Lee made heavy assaults on both ends of this line, but the tough and seasoned Army of the Potomac

beat them off, often in the most brutal hand-to-hand fighting.

The climax of the battle came the next day, July 3, when 15,000 rebels under George Pickett lined up for a frontal assault on the Union center. (At this moment, far to the west, Grant and Confederate General John Pemberton were discussing the surrender of the Vicksburg garrison.) Pickett's columns surged forward and briefly breached the Union center, but Meade's men hurled them back.

These fateful days in July, 1863, sealed the doom of the Confederacy. On July 4, Vicksburg capitulated, soon to be followed by Port Hudson 250 miles downriver. As Lincoln said, "The Father of Waters goes unvexed to the sea." The Confederacy was split in two. On July 5, Lee set his mangled army on the roads back to Virginia, his 17-mile-long wagon train of frightfully wounded men leaving a trail of shocked horror through the once peaceful countryside. Desperately hurt men swamped Gettysburg and nearby towns, and a Quaker nurse admitted, "There are no words in the English language to express the suffering I have witnessed today."

But one man was able to give expression to it, and also to the Civil War's ultimate meaning. In November, at the dedication of the Gettysburg military cemetery, a tall, ungainly man from the Illinois prairie spoke for all "the brave men, living and dead," who had fought, and were to fight, on the battlefields of that war.

MEMORIAL HALL LIBRARY, ANDOVER

PRESIDENT LINCOLN

Lincoln, in his message to Congress on December 1, 1862, said, "Fellow-citizens, *we* cannot escape history. We of this Congress and this administration will be remembered in spite of ourselves. No personal significance, or insignificance, can spare one or another of us. The fiery trial through which we pass will light us down, in honor or dishonor, to the latest generation." It is almost exactly in the sense that Lincoln stated that we remember the Civil War and particularly his place in it. The war was the beginning of a conflict we are still trying to resolve, in the North and the South, as we attempt to honor the equality this country promises. Today, Lincoln is seen as the embodiment of that struggle, and he is remembered as a man who fought and died to preserve the Union and make equality live for all.

655

IN WASHINGTON

LIBRARY OF CONGRESS

At Lincoln's first inauguration on March 4, 1861, the Capitol dome was still a half-completed shell and Lincoln an untried politician who had taken on some of the most complex responsibilities any American President had faced. In fighting to restore the Union, he had little time for anything but the great struggle that as President he had officially begun, and few moments like the imagined one at the left. The engraving shows his wife Mary, two sons—Robert, in uniform, and Tad—and a portrait of Willie, a son who had died at the age of 12. Below is one of the few social events during the war— a reception held for Ulysses S. Grant, who stands to the left of the President.

NEW-YORK HISTORICAL SOCIETY

COLLECTION OF WINSLOW CARLTON—FRANCIS G. MAYER

MARYLAND HISTORICAL SOCIETY

LINCOLN
IN CARTOONS

Few Presidents have been the subject of so many cartoons, but few have had a physical appearance so easily caricatured and have been involved in questions about which such controversy raged. At the left, Lincoln, dressed as the all-powerful knight under whose foot is the Constitution, the law, and habeas corpus, contemplates a paper marked Defeat. Below, in a symbolic 1862 painting by D. G. Blythe, Lincoln, chained to strict constitutional behavior by Tammany Hall Democrats, is handicapped in his efforts to destroy the fierce dragon of rebellion.

M. AND M. KAROLIK COLLECTION, MUSEUM OF FINE ARTS, BOSTON

To a French cartoonist, Lincoln appears so powerful in his own country that he holds Uncle Sam in his hand and looks at him through a magnifying glass. To the left and below are two comments on Lincoln's election victory in 1864: Long Lincoln becomes even longer, and a giant Majority carries him through the election waters.

COLLECTION OF MRS. JOHN NICHOLAS BROWN

PRESIDENT LINCOLN

THE ACHIEVEMENTS

COLLECTION OF ART AND SCULPTURE, FOREST LAWN MEMORIAL-PARK

Although what Lincoln accomplished as President was largely related to the Civil War, it was such a crucial part of America's history that his deep involvement only certifies to his greatness. The symbolic painting at the upper left shows his attempt at reconciliation between the North and the South. At the left, Lincoln reads the Emancipation Proclamation to his cabinet on July 22, 1862. The document was important in rallying the North's support of the war, but it also took a stand for the Union against the injustice of slavery. Above is a painting of the delivery of the Gettysburg Address, by Fletcher C. Ransome. The speech lasted but a few minutes, and only later was it recognized as the great statement of the principles of the Union. At the right is Lincoln at City Point, Virginia, being welcomed by his troops and by the liberated slaves. The North's victory was in no small measure a result of his leadership.

BETTMAN ARCHIVE

LIBRARY OF CONGRESS

CULVER PICTURES

BOTH: NEW-YORK HISTORICAL SOCIETY

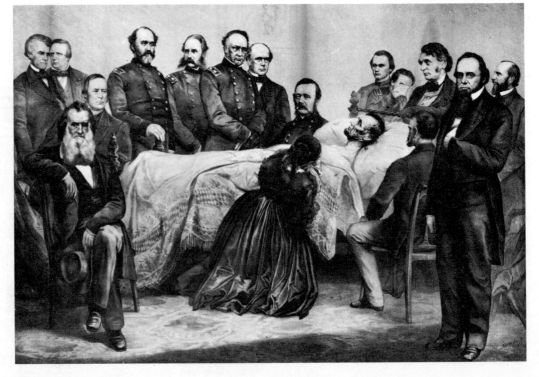

THE MURDER

On April 14, 1865—Good Friday—John Wilkes Booth, an actor then 26, entered Ford's Theatre, where Lincoln and his wife were watching a play titled *Our American Cousin.* He went to Lincoln's box just as the President's bodyguard left to get a drink. Booth opened the door quietly, stepped into the box, and shot Lincoln in the back of the head (left). In a matter of seconds, Booth was on a horse he had waiting at the stage door. Lincoln did not live long; he died the next morning (left, bottom). The search began for the murderer and his co-conspirators, with a $100,000 reward offered (right). On April 26, Booth, who had injured his leg, was shot as he moved toward the door of a barn that had been set on fire by cavalrymen who had found him (below).

NEW-YORK HISTORICAL SOCIETY

HARRY T. PETERS COLLECTION, MUSEUM OF THE CITY OF NEW YORK

TRIBUTE
AND TOLL

Lincoln's funeral cortege was a spectacle that reaffirmed his importance to the nation. His body was taken from city to city on the way to Springfield, Illinois, where it was buried. Below, the procession passes through New York City. At the left, Lincoln is posed beside Washington, over the words "The Father and the Savior of Our Country." At the right is his last photograph, showing the toll the Presidency took after the portrait at the beginning of this portfolio was drawn.

COLLECTION OF MRS. JOHN NICHOLAS BROWN

COLLECTION OF FREDERICK HILL MESERVE

COLLECTION OF JAY P. ALTMAYER

CHAPTER 23

ROAD TO VICTORY

The military aspect of the Civil War has always attracted the most attention. The roar of gunfire, the massed movements of uniformed men, the shrill of bugles, and the drama of hand-to-hand combat have fascinated students of warfare for a century. Behind the lines, however, life was less spectacular. It was the story of backbreaking labor to provide the fighting men with food and arms, of nerve-tingling uncertainty about the course of national events, of heartbreak over sons or brothers or husbands lost in battle. If the men on the firing lines won the victories, the means to those victories were forged on the home front.

Never in the nation's history had Americans worked harder for victory than in the Civil War. Northerners and Southerners alike threw themselves into the task of supplying their respective armies. Both governments made tremendous demands upon civil-

Robert E. Lee, commander of the Army of Northern Virginia for the major part of the war, was a brilliant military strategist. He, almost by himself, was responsible for the South's many victories against the Union's greater forces and supplies.

ians and, in general, received willing cooperation.

By 1863, the Northern war economy was rumbling along in high gear. Everything from steamboats to shovels was needed—and produced. Denied Southern cotton, textile mills turned to wool for blankets and uniforms. Hides by the hundreds of thousands were turned into shoes and harness and saddles; ironworks manufactured locomotives, ordnance, armor plate. Where private enterprise lagged, the government set up its own factories or arsenals. Agriculture boomed, with machinery doing the job of farm workers drawn into the army. King Wheat replaced King Cotton in the lexicon of foreign trade.

In short, everything that a nation needed to fight a modern war was produced in uncounted numbers. Inevitably there were profiteers with gold-headed canes and flamboyant diamond stickpins, but for every crooked tycoon there were thousands of ordinary citizens living on fixed incomes who did their best to cope with rising prices and still make a contribution to the war effort. Those who could bought financier Jay Cooke's war bonds; others knitted, sewed, nursed, or lent any other assistance in their power.

Life behind the Confederate lines was grimmer. At the outbreak of the war, the South was pitifully short of everything but good fighting men, and its economy moved backward at an accelerating pace as the conflict went on. Confederate currency, unbacked by a gold reserve, became worth less and less, until by the end of 1864 it was worth nothing at all. Although the South managed to keep its fighting men in weapons for four years (with a good part of those weapons captured from federal troops), it was hard-pressed to feed and clothe them. During the war, the Confederacy produced not a single mile of railroad track,

COLLECTION OF MRS. JOHN NICHOLAS BROWN

The South's main source of income, cotton, was often captured and sold to England by Northerners, as cartooned above. Another problem was her currency (below), which was never declared legal tender. Patriotism alone gave it value.

STACK'S COINS

A recruiting scene in the North shows that the main appeal of the federal government was not to the patriotism of its men, but to their pocketbook.

and its antiquated transportation system was wholly incapable of the load it was asked to bear.

Southern citizens demonstrated the meaning of "total war" long before the term came into popular use. Few armies in world history have had more support and loyalty from the populace than those of the Confederate states. Southerners put their beliefs on the line, and gave until there was no more to give.

Finding soldiers to man the firing lines became increasingly difficult as the war dragged on. At first, volunteers made up the armies of both sides, but men who choose to go to war usually turn up where the fighting is heaviest. As a result, the ranks of the volunteers were soon decimated,

and both North and South turned to a military draft. The Confederacy's draft laws were reasonably fair, and on the whole its system was successful. But in the North the system was an atrocity. A man could pay to avoid the draft, or he could hire a substitute to go to war in his place. These substitutes were often the dregs of society, of no use whatever to the army.

The bounty system was another attempt to meet this problem. A sizable cash payment was offered to enlist (and, incidentally, avoid the draft). All that this proved, however, was that men who joined the army for money were seldom inclined to risk their lives. The system also produced a large number of bounty jumpers—men who accepted their bounty, de-

In Richmond's Libby Prison, over 1,000 Union officers were confined in eight rooms, like the one in David Blythe's painting, in an old tobacco warehouse.

serted at the first opportunity, rejoined for another bounty at another location, and repeated the whole process as long as they could evade detection.

Perhaps nothing more quickly dispels the romantic gloss sometimes applied to the Civil War than the story of the prisoner-of-war camps. These deathtraps lay like festering sores across the land, both North and South. In places such as Andersonville in Georgia, Libby Prison in Richmond, Camp Douglas near Chicago, and Elmira Prison in New York, men died like flies from untreated wounds,

from starvation, and from any number of diseases. The statistics are appalling: Of the 400,000 imprisoned, nearly 50,000 died, and uncounted thousands suffered crippling ailments from which they never fully recovered. This was seldom the result of any conscious policy of brutality; prisoners simply succumbed to neglect, to bureaucratic inefficiency, to the heartlessness of war.

The industrial boom, the profiteers, the bounty jumpers, the prison camps, the sacrifices of the people at home—they were all threads of the fabric of a society torn by a civil war and changed forever. And no portion of that society was more radically changed than the "peculiar institution" of slavery. By 1863, the institution was visibly crumbling, thanks to the federal armies. General Sherman, returning from a raid in Mississippi, reported, "We bring in some 500 prisoners, a good many refugees, and about 10 miles of Negroes."

Many Northern soldiers had enlisted both to save the Union and destroy slavery. Others thought of the Union alone and cared little for the slaves. But all obeyed army orders, and if it was army policy to strip Southern plantations of their labor supply, they had little choice but to go along. The destruction of slavery was nowhere more evident than in the Mississippi Valley in 1863; then it became plain in the Eastern theater in 1864 as the Union Army began to penetrate deeply into the Confederacy.

Forcing the gateway

The armies of Lee and Meade in the East were exhausted after Gettysburg, and for the rest of 1863 they sparred and probed at each other to little effect. In addition, both generals had to feed men into the rapidly expanding cockpit of war in eastern Tennessee.

Even as Grant closed the ring on Vicksburg, and Lee marched to his fateful clash at Gettysburg, Rosecrans was pushing southward with the

M. AND M. KAROLIK COLLECTION, MUSEUM OF FINE ARTS, BOSTON

COLLECTION OF C. C. TRAVIS

Closing in on Chattanooga, the federal forces crossed the Tennessee River near Stevenson, Alabama. General Rosecrans is at the left, waving his sword.

671

COLLECTION OF LLOYD OSTENDORF

LIBRARY OF CONGRESS

COOK COLLECTION, VALENTINE MUSEUM

William S. Rosecrans   *George H. Thomas*   *Braxton Bragg*

Army of the Cumberland. His goal was Chattanooga, the logical railroad base for any thrust into the Deep South. After a skillful campaign of maneuver, Rosecrans forced Bragg's Confederate Army of Tennessee out of Chattanooga and occupied the city on September 9.

The bulk of the federal army, however, was wandering around in the mountainous country of northern Georgia, trying to come to grips with Bragg's force. On September 19, the two armies met in the gloomy woodlands around Chickamauga Creek, a dozen miles south of Chattanooga. The fighting on the 19th was indecisive, but the next day James Longstreet—who had been sent west with two divisions from Lee's army—punched a hole in the Union center and split Rosecrans' army in half. Most of the routed Federals and their commanding officer fled toward Chattanooga, but Major General George H. Thomas pulled enough men together to stand off the heavy Southern assaults. On that day Thomas earned a nickname, the Rock of Chickamauga, and bought enough time for the rest of the army to escape.

Chickamauga was the only important victory the Confederacy ever won in the Western theater—and Bragg proceeded to throw it away. Despite the pleadings of his officers, he let Rosecrans establish himself solidly in Chattanooga. The Southerner was content to occupy Missionary Ridge, overlooking the city, and try to starve the Federals into surrender.

The high command in Washington was spurred into action. Heavy reinforcements were dispatched from Meade's army in Virginia and Sherman's force in Memphis. Rosecrans was replaced by Thomas, and Grant

COLLECTION OF C. C. TRAVIS

The Union and rebel forces met at Chickamauga on September 20, 1863. They were painted by William Travis as if locked in a fierce hand-to-hand combat.

was made supreme commander in the Western theater.

The first task was to open a supply line to beleaguered Chattanooga, which Grant and Thomas started to do. Now that they could again "board at home," as President Lincoln wrote, the Federals should attempt to break Bragg's siege lines. On November 25, 1863, this was done, by the soldiers of the Army of the Cumberland operating wholly on their own. These men had been humiliated by their defeat at Chickamauga and mercilessly derided by the reinforcements sent to "rescue" them, and they were fighting mad. They delivered, on orders, a feint at Missionary Ridge; then, without orders, they charged directly up the steep face of the ridge and sent Bragg's Confederates reeling into Georgia.

The fight at Missionary Ridge had momentous results. The North now had a springboard from which to launch a thrust into the heart of the Confederacy. William T. Sherman, newly appointed to command the Western theater, would lead this thrust. Most important, U. S. Grant was brought to Washington and named general-in-chief of all the Union armies. At last, after two and a half years of fighting, the federal war machine was to be directed by a soldier who knew exactly what he wanted to do and how to do it. This stocky, quiet man who looked, a fellow officer said, "as if he had determined to drive his head through a brick wall, and was about to do it" now began to forge a strategy that was to win the war for the North.

The Union offensive

As Grant saw it, the problem was deceptively simple. The Confederacy had two main armies—Lee's Army of

673

Hooker's capture of Lookout Mountain was more dramatic than decisive, and Grant regarded

OFFICE OF THE CHIEF OF MILITARY HISTORY, U.S. ARMY

it simply as a first step in his general assault on Bragg's main Missionary Ridge line.

Northern Virginia encamped below the Rapidan River in Virginia, and the Army of Tennessee, now commanded by General Joseph E. Johnston (Bragg finally having been relieved), lying in north Georgia. The Confederate States of America could exist only as long as these two armies existed. Johnston was Sherman's assignment; Grant himself would travel with the Army of the Potomac against Lee. In May, 1864, the Federals began to move south.

Grant crossed the Rapidan and tried to march quickly through the Wilderness to turn Lee's flank. But the wily Confederate once more chose to make the Wilderness his battlefield. There ensued a desperate struggle in the tangled underbrush, with the acrid battle smoke hanging low under the treetops. It was, a Union soldier wrote, "simply bushwhacking on a grand scale." When the musketry sputtered out on May 6 after two days of fighting, Lee had won another victory, smashing in both ends of the federal line and inflicting 17,500 casualties at a cost of 8,000.

Grant shrugged off the defeat and pushed on southward. Lee managed to block his path at Spotsylvania

William Mahone's Confederate forces counterattack at Petersburg after the North had made several attempts to break through the Confederate defenses, but hard-fighting Mahone could do no more than re-establish his position.

Court House, and for 12 days the two armies slashed at each other.

On one of those days, May 12, the fighting reached a new pitch of intensity. Grant launched a powerful punch at the Confederate center, broke through, and then was held by counterattacks. For 18 solid hours, in a pelting rain, men in blue and gray killed one another at point-blank range at a spot in the Southern line known simply as Bloody Angle.

Grant finally broke off the action at Spotsylvania and continued his flanking operation. Once more the two armies conducted a nightmare race, aiming for the strategically important crossroads hamlet of Cold Harbor, east of Richmond. Grant again attempted a frontal attack and again failed, losing 7,000 men in 30 minutes. A Southern officer observed that the dead "covered more than five acres of ground about as thickly as they could be laid."

In a month of steady fighting, Grant's losses averaged 2,000 men a day, and anguished Northerners began calling him The Butcher. But that stubborn warrior, with grim logic, knew he could make his losses good while Lee could not.

Grant now changed his tactics and made a swift skillful flanking march past Richmond and across the James. His target was Petersburg, 20 miles

COMMONWEALTH CLUB, RICHMOND

Ulysses S. Grant, photographed at City Point, Virginia, during the siege of Petersburg, was then a lieutenant general.

NATIONAL ARCHIVES

677

The Confederacy surrounded the city of Atlanta with strong lines of forti-fications, even stripping the frame houses of their lumber to build trenches.

south of Richmond, through which passed nearly all the railroad lines that supplied both the Confederate capital and Lee's army.

The advance elements of the Army of the Potomac arrived before Petersburg on June 15. For once in his career, Robert E. Lee had been fooled, and his army was a day's march away. With a golden chance staring him in the face, the officer in charge of the Union spearhead bungled his attack on the thinly manned Petersburg fortifications. Then Lee's veterans arrived, and the chance was gone. The Federals settled down to lay siege.

Meanwhile, in Georgia, Sherman was fighting a different kind of war. He and Johnston moved crabwise across the northern half of the state,

OLD PRINT SHOP

COLLECTION OF FREDERICK HILL MESERVE

William Tecumseh Sherman

Sherman, after taking Atlanta, went on his famous March to the Sea, burning houses and tearing up the railway lines he crossed.

thrusting, parrying, seeking an opening. On June 27, Sherman tried a frontal attack on the Confederates at Kennesaw Mountain and was beaten back with severe losses. He resumed his flanking operations. By mid-July, Johnston's outnumbered army was in the fortifications of Atlanta, a key manufacturing and transportation center. Sherman prepared for a siege.

Grant's strategy had succeeded in pinning down the two Confederate armies, but this fact was not quite clear to war-weary Northerners. All they could see was that no great victories had been won, and that the casualty lists were reaching proportions undreamed of in those far-off days of 1861. Abraham Lincoln was facing reelection in November, and he began

to feel he could not win. If he should lose, a negotiated peace would almost surely follow, with the South becoming an independent nation.

Closing the ring

Some people in the South—including General Johnston—saw quite clearly the problem Lincoln faced. To Johnston it seemed unlikely that the Confederacy could any longer win independence by military means; he felt that the only hope was to prolong the war until the North became tired of the death and destruction, repudiated Lincoln, and sued for peace. Jefferson Davis, however, saw things differently. To Davis, a military man himself, only military victories counted. In his view, Johnston had failed to fight. On July 17, 1864, he replaced Johnston with General John Bell Hood.

Hood was an impetuous Texan whose specialty was hard, head-to-head fighting. He had commanded superb assault troops under Lee, and had lost the use of an arm at Gettysburg and a leg at Chickamauga. As Sherman pressed his 100,000-man force on Atlanta, Hood went over to the attack.

On July 20, he hit the Federals as they crossed Peachtree Creek north of the city, but he was up against George Thomas, and Thomas threw him back. Hood tried again two days later in what was called the Battle of Atlanta. Once more he was stopped. On July 28, Hood launched a third assault, west of Atlanta at Ezra Church, only

COOK COLLECTION, VALENTINE MUSEUM

Jubal A. Early

Early made a surprise attack on Sheridan on October 19, 1864, just 20 miles south of Winchester, Virginia, and until Sheridan rallied his panic-stricken men (right), they were frantically retreating.

to be driven back with heavy losses. The city was now ringed on three sides, and the Confederate forces had to get out or be trapped. On September 2, Atlanta was occupied by federal troops. The Lincoln administration could at last announce a major victory.

At Petersburg, in that summer of 1864, a war of attrition was under way. Lee's entrenchments were too strong to break with frontal assaults, and Grant had to be content to use his superior manpower to extend his lines gradually, stretching the already thin gray ranks. It was pointed out to

COLLECTION OF MRS. JOHN NICHOLAS BROWN

Grant that the campaign resembled the Kilkenny cats that devoured each other. He admitted there was some truth to this, but added, "Our cat has the longer tail."

In desperation, Lee once more tried the tactic of threatening Washington. He sent hard-bitten Jubal A. Early and a small striking force north into the Shenandoah Valley. In July, Early tried a quick thrust at Washington, but he was blocked by the army corps that Grant quickly dispatched to the capital. As Early withdrew, Grant determined to take the Shenandoah Valley out of the war for good. This

would not only close off Lee's favorite invasion route, but it would also eliminate a major source of food and forage for the Confederate forces. The job was given to a bandy-legged, hard-as-nails cavalryman named Philip Sheridan.

In September, Sheridan, pushing Early's outnumbered force before him, began to lay waste to the valley. Barns and corncribs and mills went up in smoke, livestock was slaughtered or driven away, and whole families—many of them pro-Union—were forced to evacuate their homes. This was total war. On October 19, Early auda-

NATIONAL PARK SERVICE MUSEUM, APPOMATTOX

April 9, 1865, Lee surrendered his army to Grant at Appomatox Court House.
The broadside below appeared in Detroit, expressing the joy of peace at last.

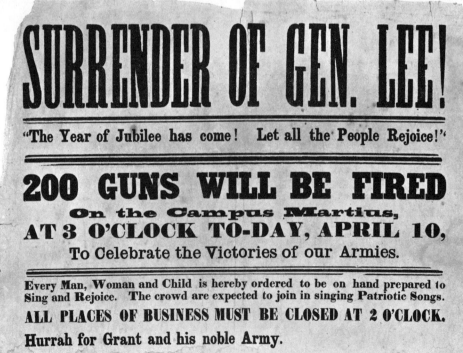

BURTON HISTORICAL COLLECTION, DETROIT PUBLIC LIBRARY

COLLECTION OF ALEXANDER MCCOOK CRAIGHEAD

682

ciously attacked Sheridan's army at Cedar Creek, but with Sheridan himself rallying the surprised Federals, the Confederates were completely shattered and driven for good from the Shenandoah Valley.

The Democrats had nominated General George McClellan to oppose the President in the election. But between McClellan's nomination in August and the election in November, Sherman and Sheridan had dramatically put the federal war machine on the road to victory. The President was overwhelmingly re-elected. "I earnestly believe that the consequences of this day's work," Lincoln said, "will be to the lasting advantage, if not to the very salvation, of the country."

Triumph and tragedy

In Georgia in November there occurred one of the strangest scenes of the Civil War. Sherman and Hood turned their backs on each other and marched off in different directions. Hood gambled on one throw of the dice, driving north into Tennessee and hoping Sherman would follow. Sherman was delighted. "If he will go to the Ohio River, I'll give him rations,"

Grant's dispatch—"General Lee surrendered the Army of Northern Virginia this afternoon on terms proposed by myself"—brought the North scenes like this.

he announced. The Union general sent reinforcements to General Thomas at Nashville, burned a sizable part of Atlanta, and set about taking the State of Georgia out of the war.

Sherman's army, virtually unopposed, slashed a 60-mile-wide path of devastation from Atlanta to the sea. His men lived high off the land, burning or destroying what they could not eat or carry away. On the fringes of the army, deserters and riffraff known as bummers looted and burned dwellings as well. The March to the Sea was a grim lesson to the Confederacy that it could no longer defend its heartland, and it left an unhealing wound on the South. On December 22, Sherman seized Savannah and a great hoard of military supplies. He whimsically wired Lincoln, offering the city as a Christmas present.

Meanwhile, Hood's Army of Tennessee was on its last march. On November 30, at Franklin, Tennessee, the Confederates made a frontal attack not unlike Pickett's charge at Gettysburg. They were slaughtered. Undaunted, Hood moved on to Nashville. There on December 15 and 16, George Thomas completely shattered the rebel army. The war in the West was over.

As 1864 became 1865, the Confederacy writhed in its death throes. Fort Fisher, guarding Wilmington, North Carolina, was captured by the Federals, closing the South's last door to the outside world. Sherman invaded South Carolina, burning and

destroying as he went, and by March he was in North Carolina. In reality, the Confederacy existed now only in the person of Robert E. Lee and his beleaguered army at Petersburg.

In the first days of April, Grant broke through the Southerner's defenses. Lee evacuated Petersburg and Richmond and tried to get his army away to the West. Scenting victory, the long-suffering Army of the Potomac pursued vigorously. On April 9, at Appomattox Court House, Lee surrendered his starving and exhausted troops to Grant.

The Civil War had lasted almost exactly four years. It had cost over 600,000 lives (more than all of the nation's other wars combined), and wreaked incalculable damage on the land. But there remained one more scene to be acted out before the curtain came down on the American tragedy.

Abraham Lincoln had a vision of America, and he had stood in the center of the caldron of war to defend that vision. Somehow he forged the diverse and conflicting elements in the North into a force that in the end was triumphant. Then, on the night of April 14, 1865, at Ford's Theatre in Washington, an insane actor named John Wilkes Booth, professing allegiance to the Southern cause that he lacked the courage to fight for, mortally wounded the President. Lincoln died the next morning, and Secretary of War Edwin Stanton intoned, "Now he belongs to the ages."

MARINERS MUSEUM

THE NAVAL WAR

The battles on sea and river were an important part of the Civil War. First and foremost, they affected the South's economy and war materials. At the start of the conflict, the North began a blockade of the South's ports, keeping her cotton from going out and foreign military supplies from coming in. The North's eventual success in this effort was one of the main reasons for her victory, as it weakened the South economically and curtailed her ability to wage war. The battles were also a deciding factor in the action along the Mississippi River. They cut into the South's supply lines and damaged her deepest positions of strength, the loss of which often affected the pride that was so much a part of her reason for fighting. Finally, the naval war had meaning for the future of America. In both the North and the South, inventors applied their imagination to creating new forms of ship warfare. Ironclads, submarines, and torpedoes were put into use. The lack of metals and machinery in the South limited the scope of her inventions, but in the end they, too, became a part of the greater might of the united nation that was to come.

THE MAKESHIFT NAVY

St. George, Bermuda, enjoyed a wartime boom as a result of the Union blockade of the South. Here and in Nassau, cargoes from Europe were transferred from the ocean-going vessels to trimmer and faster blockade-runners for the final dash to the rebel ports.

M. AND M. KAROLIK COLLECTION, MUSEUM OF FINE ARTS, BOSTON

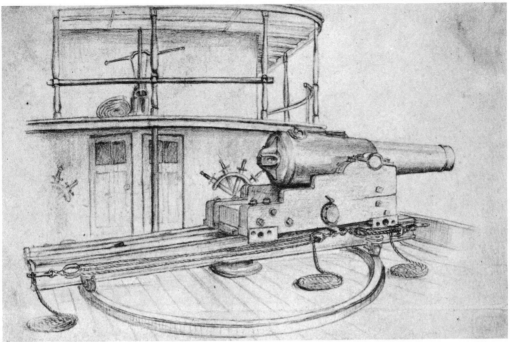

The above Mississippi River side-wheeler was first sunk by the Union Navy, then raised by it and made into a gunboat.

In 1861, Alex Simplot sketched the metamorphosis of the ferryboat *New Era* from a pleasure craft into a light-draft gunboat.

COLLECTION OF ALEXANDER McCOOK CRAIGHEAD

STATE HISTORICAL SOCIETY OF WISCONSIN

THE NEW NAVY

LIBRARY OF CONGRESS

KENNEDY GALLERIES

Swedish immigrant John Ericsson designed the Union ironclad *Monitor* that was launched January 30, 1862, on the very same day as the *Merrimack*.

COLLECTION OF OLIVER JENSEN

CHICAGO HISTORICAL SOCIETY

On March 8, the *Merrimack,* the South's ironclad, encountered Union ships, sinking the *Cumberland* and burning the *Congress*. On the next day, she (above, center) met the *Monitor* at Hampton Roads, where from eight in the morning until noon the ships battled, sometimes even touching each other, until the *Merrimack* retired, with the *Monitor* undamaged.

Commanded by Henry Walke, the federal gunboat *Carondelet* (above) was one of the eight ironclads James B. Eads built in St. Louis in 100 days with 4,000 men.

Below is Alex Simplot's painting of the brief, savage naval battle at Memphis. Of eight lightly armed and armored Confederate ships, only one escaped.

INVENTIONS

There had been earlier attempts at designing a submarine, but it was not until Horace L. Hunley brought his frail, cigar-shaped iron boiler on a flatcar to Charleston in the summer of 1863 that the idea became a reality in war. There were many unsuccessful trials—20 men were killed, including Hunley—before a submarine, the *Hunley* (above), was launched on February 17, 1864. She sank a Union ship, but she and her crew also went down.

SUBMARINE LIBRARY, GENERAL DYNAMICS CORPORATION

NEW-YORK HISTORICAL SOCIETY

CONFEDERATE MUSEUM

NEW YORK PUBLIC LIBRARY

At the top is a Confederate mine that was made from a converted beer keg, and, under it, is John Ericsson's design for an armored turret. A Union impression of the *Hunley,* with the crew too large, is shown opposite. Below is the Dahlgren gun, with curved walls meant to keep it from exploding.

COLLECTION OF JULIA B. POTTS

THE NAVAL WAR

BATTLES

Island No. 10, a Confederate fort on the Kentucky-Tennessee border of the Mississippi, surrendered to the Union Navy on April 7, 1862, after a month's bombardment by ironclads (left) and mortar boats.

At Vicksburg, Mississippi (below), Admiral David Porter's fleet ran past the city's guns on the night of April 16, 1863. On July 4, 1863, General Grant, moving in from the south, captured the city.

MARINERS MUSEUM

CHICAGO HISTORICAL SOCIETY

In one of the major battles of the war, the U.S.S. *Kearsarge,* under the command of Captain John A. Winslow, sank the rebel raider *Alabama* near Cherbourg, France, where she had gone for repairs.

OVERLEAF: On the morning of August 5, 1864, Admiral David Farrugut moved into Mobile Bay, his flagship *Hartford* deluged by gunfire, but by 10 o'clock that same morning he had taken the port.

WADSWORTH ATHENEUM

CHAPTER 24

RECONSTRUCTION

On May 23 and 24, 1865, Americans and representatives from foreign lands crowded along Washington's Pennsylvania Avenue to watch the Grand Review. On the first day, General George Meade led the neat, seemingly endless ranks of the veteran Army of the Potomac on parade, before the admiring eyes of the excited crowds. Then, on the following day, Sherman's rough and ready Westerners, fresh from their history-making march through a shattered South, slouched along the avenue behind their grizzled leader. Washington was solidly decked with colored bunting and aflutter with thousands of flags. The holiday spirit was everywhere apparent. A scattering of empty sleeves and an occasional peg leg were about all that reminded the people of the grim past. The war was over, and to them the future was bright.

All across Dixie silence hung like a death pall. Soldiers came home quietly, grimly, to a tearful welcome. Their farms, their homes, their former

One of the themes of the United States centennial, as shown on this allegorical sheet-music cover, was the solidarity of the Union.

CULVER PICTURES

places of business frequently lay in ruins. Members of their families were often missing. The land and the people were exhausted from the protracted struggle.

Ahead lay an uncertain future. What would be the penalty for losing, and what sort of existence would the days ahead provide? These were the big questions. The South would be rebuilt, would live again and grow again. But under what conditions? Tight-lipped, Southerners waited to find out. All eyes were fixed upon Washington, upon Congress, and upon the new President from Tennessee, Andrew Johnson.

Americans discovered, in the years immediately following 1865, that the problems of peace were more complex than those of war. In the military conflict, violent and bloody as it had been, the road ahead was often well marked. The problems of peace were more subtle, more complex, more disturbing. They called for judgment, fairness, and thoughtful consideration, at a time when wartime passions still ran high. In 1865, hatreds smoldered, memories of personal losses were burned deeply into men's minds, and peace without revenge was hard to envisage.

The first postwar decade is usually referred to as the reconstruction era. Like so many terms, it does not correctly or completely describe or explain. It was not possible, in 1865, simply to reconstruct the United States as it had existed in 1861. The states were reassembled and called united, but the result was more than a repair job. It was a new nation.

Certainly the Old South was no more. Its labor base, slavery, was demolished and the day of the great plantation was gone. This did not mean that growing cotton would stop or that black farmers would not grow it. But the plantation ideal—the Bourbon aristocrat at the top and slave labor at work in the fields—was a thing of the past. Cotton now would be grown by both whites and blacks as sharecroppers, and a system of tenancy would replace the old ways of slavery.

Like the South, the North could not be reconstructed to resemble its former self. Men of 1861 returned from the war fronts in 1865 to a newly industrialized and much more centralized country. Wartime demands for efficiency produced an era of expansion and consolidation that would continue throughout the century. The steel age was at hand, with its huge factories and its enormous productive capacity. The Homestead Act of 1862, coupled with wartime requirements for food, had revolutionized agricul-

ture. Farmers, blessed by high prices and presented with government lands, spent their money freely for farm machinery. In a single spurt, in just a few years, the North shot decades ahead of the South in agricultural development.

Moreover, there could be no reconstruction from a political standpoint. For the time being—indeed, until the election of Woodrow Wilson in 1912 —the United States was virtually a one-party nation. The only Democratic President between Buchanan and Wilson was Grover Cleveland. Except for Cleveland's two-term interruption, the Republicans had things pretty much their own way. It would take the Democratic Party more than a generation to recover its former strength.

Even those who ran the federal government could not agree upon the meaning of reconstruction. Lincoln believed it meant readjusting and realigning the Southern states to put them back into the Union. At no time did the President ever recognize the validity of secession. He took the view that these states had never left the Union, that they were, in a sense, merely "kidnapped" by individuals in arms against the government.

A number of Congressmen, including many members of Lincoln's own Republican Party, did not agree with him. They felt that it was impossible to "put Humpty Dumpty together again." These hardheaded Radical Republicans held that the Southern

BETTMAN ARCHIVE

Peace had been signed in April, 1865, and the troops had begun to return home, but on May 23 and 24, seemingly endless columns of men marched down Washington's Pennsylvania Avenue as the Union Army paraded in its final review.

"erring sisters" had left home for good and therefore had lost all former rights and privileges. To a large block of Republicans, the South was merely a conquered province, to be treated as one of the spoils of war.

The American people, as a whole, were eager for some kind of settlement. The majority looked forward to no more than the return of peace and "the good old days." In the North, there was a strong desire to reduce the large army and thereby weaken the power of the military regime that had controlled the country during the war. Civil justice had suffered in this period, and that fact went against the Anglo-Saxon tradition. Northerners also wanted to lower taxes as quickly as possible. In all these things, they anticipated a return to what they had known before. But this is something no postwar generation has ever been able to find.

Presidential reconstruction

Despite the wish to recapture peace and prosperity, the question of how to treat the conquered South remained the burning issue. Long before the war ended, there was talk about how the vanquished should be treated when the final gun had been fired. It was discussed as early as 1862. In December,

1863, Lincoln proposed that when one-tenth of the qualified Southern voters for the year 1860 took an oath of loyalty to the Constitution, they might set up a state government and ask for recognition by the federal government. This so-called One-Tenth Plan or Lincoln Plan (also referred to as the Louisiana Plan) assumed that at all times there had remained some loyal people in the South—people who never had lost their rights as Americans. Through the use of his Presidential power of pardon, Lincoln proposed to restore their full rights to them. Those who were sorry could say so and would then be invited to return to the fold.

Lincoln's plan, announced at the height of the war, revealed his desire to show the world that the rebellion was coming to an end. A gradual re-entrance of states into the Union would be strong proof. In 1864, Louisiana and Arkansas and, in 1865, Tennessee held conventions and established loyal governments under the new plan. The furious Radicals in Congress were convinced that this meant a soft peace.

When Lincoln was assassinated, those who had opposed his plans for

This mowing machine was one of the many new inventions in the mid-19th century that was turning America into a land of agricultural and industrial wealth.

the South took new hope. The man whose credo was "With malice toward none; with charity for all" was dead, and in his place was Andrew Johnson, a Tennessee Unionist who had taken a pronounced stand against those in rebellion. Benjamin Wade, the militant Senator from Ohio, spoke for his Radical friends when he said, "Johnson, we have faith in you! By the gods, there will be no trouble now in running the government!"

Those who had hoped for a violently anti-Southern stand by Johnson were disappointed, however. His earlier sentiment that "treason is a crime and must be punished as a crime" was replaced by moderation and an almost complete acceptance of Lincoln's viewpoint.

Congress recessed soon after Johnson's accession to the Presidency. From April until December, when the next regular session convened, the members were at home. During their absence, Johnson took full advantage of the situation. Closely following Lincoln's earlier procedure, but making its stipulations slightly more strict, the new President reopened the doors of the Union. By December, 1865, all the seceded states but Texas had returned to the fold. When Congress met again, its members were amazed to find Southerners who had fought the Union only months before waiting to claim their seats.

Members of the Republican Party had more at stake than merely making a hard peace with the South. Before the war, under the provisions in Article I of the Constitution, only three-fifths of the slave population was counted for Congressional representation. Now, with thousands of slaves at liberty, the black was no longer three-fifths of a person politically, but counted as one. This would mean at least 12 additional Southern representatives in Congress. It is small wonder that the Radical Republicans were disturbed at the sudden return of the recalcitrant states. It meant they would have no opportunity to exercise any control over the South. It meant also that the Southerners were back, stronger than ever, in the halls of Congress. Republicans anxiously cast about for some way to deny them their seats.

Congressional reconstruction

An ancient rule came to the rescue of the Northern Congressmen, and through its application they took command of the reconstruction problem. Congress may pass upon the qualifications of its own members, excluding those who are deemed unfit to join the club. Radical Republicans seized upon this device to hold off the newly elected Southern members. It was a desperate move, one lacking in honesty and fairness, but those who invoked it were afraid that unless they took the initiative at that point, all would be lost.

The Radicals did not try to disqualify the Southerners permanently. They appointed a committee, made up

OLD PRINT SHOP

Benjamin F. Wade   Thaddeus Stevens   Edwin M. Stanton

*Wade, Stevens, and Stanton were all members of the Radical wing of the
Republican Party, which after the Civil War refused to accept the moderate
measures for the reconstruction of the South that were instituted by Lincoln
before his death and in part continued by his successor, Andrew Johnson.*

of six Senators and nine Representatives, to study the matter. The delay would allow time to strengthen Republican Party lines and to make plans. Yet the move was more than a mere stalling measure. Led by vindictive Thaddeus Stevens of Pennsylvania, the group constituted a permanent committee on reconstruction. It spearheaded the Radical group in the Senate, whose members wanted sole control of the problem. The Committee of Fifteen, as it became known, was in no hurry. For six months it studied the whole question of reconstruction, of suffrage in the South, and of the status of those Southerners recently elected to Congress. During this time the unhappy applicants sat outside and waited.

The creation of Stevens' committee touched off warfare between Congress and Andrew Johnson, for its very existence challenged acceptance of the Southern states. Hostilities broke out in earnest during February, 1866, when Congress passed, and Johnson vetoed, a bill extending the Freedmen's Bureau. This organization, created originally to take care of the many newly freed slaves, was singled out by the Radicals as an instrument for firm control of blacks politically. Johnson vetoed the bill and there were not enough votes to override his veto.

Congress tried to attack the problem directly when in March it passed the Civil Rights Bill, the provisions of which not only anticipated the Fourteenth Amendment by declaring that former slaves were citizens, but threatened to punish those states that failed to recognize it. Johnson promptly exercised his veto, but this time it was overridden. In July, the Radicals passed another Freedmen's Bureau bill and then overrode Johnson's veto. With this show of strength they began to get confident.

Congress next turned its attention to the Fourteenth Amendment. Laws may be rescinded or modified rather easily, but the Constitution is harder to tamper with. Republicans were eager to secure rights for the blacks forever—not so much for humanitarian as for political reasons. The black population would account for some 30 Representatives in Congress, and there was no reason, in Republican minds, that they should not be members of that party. Here was the heart of the matter of reconstruction, from a Congressional point of view. It was an extreme stand—one that some of the conservatives in the Republican Party found hard to swallow, but to party leaders it was necessary for survival.

In writing the Fourteenth Amendment, its authors firmly imbedded into its first section the aims of the Civil Rights Act to avoid any future question of constitutionality on that score. Next they tried to force Southern states to give voting rights to blacks by threatening to reduce their representation in Congress if all male adult citizens in those states were not enfranchised. As a further blow to the South, it was provided that, unless pardoned by Congress, no supporter of the Confederacy who had formerly held a federal or state position could

Andrew Johnson

now hold office. Finally, the Confederate debt was repudiated and former masters of slaves were denied any compensation for their losses through emancipation.

Thus the Radical Congressmen tried to guarantee their notions of reconstruction by grafting them to the Constitution. The Thirteenth Amendment, which had granted all slaves the freedom earlier expressed in Lincoln's Emancipation Proclamation, was the beginning. The Fourteenth Amendment, which mentioned only voting rights for "male inhabitants," now was fortified by a Fifteenth Amendment, which specifically provided that no one should be denied the ballot because of "race, color, or previous condition of servitude." The Radicals were determined to leave no loopholes for uncooperative Southern whites to

703

slip through. The Constitution was to be the big weapon against an unfriendly state executive.

Andrew Johnson fought back, using every weapon in his power. In 1866, during the mid-term election, he toured the nation, blasting at his opponents and recommending the election of those who agreed with his position. The attempt was an utter failure, and the vote of confidence given the Radicals in their victory at the polls spurred them on to more audacious acts.

In March, 1867, Congress enacted legislation dividing the South into five military districts, each commanded by a general. The officers were to enroll all males, black and white, and administer an oath of allegiance, after which those qualified to vote would elect representatives to state constitutional conventions. Each of the states had to accept the idea of black suffrage and must approve the Fourteenth Amendment. Naturally, there were cries of "Unconstitutional," but when asked for its judgment, the Supreme Court declined to give it. This first Reconstruction Act, passed March 2, 1867, and shored up by three supplemental acts, fastened the grip of Congress upon the conquered South.

War on Capitol Hill

By the spring of 1867, the hard core of Radical Republicans in Congress were in the saddle and completely confident. By then, Presidential vetoes were laughably low hurdles to them. As chief executive, sworn to uphold the law of the land, Johnson was obliged to carry out Congressional wishes. He did his best, appointing military commanders who in turn set into motion in each of their districts

BOTH: CULVER PICTURES

the machinery of reconstruction. During the winter and spring of 1867–68, the newly elected Southern conventions labored and, except for Texas, they completed their tasks of constitution-making.

But this was not enough for the vindictive elements in Congress. Mere supremacy over Johnson was too little for men bent on ruining him. In March, 1867, on the same day the first reconstruction bill became law, Congress also passed the Tenure of Office Act. This was designed to prevent Johnson from discharging hostile appointees and replacing them with his own supporters. Johnson vetoed the bill, of course, and it was promptly passed over his veto. Undaunted, the President held that the law was unconstitutional and therefore void. The Supreme Court, at the lowest ebb in its history, maintained complete silence. Proceeding alone, Johnson ignored the Tenure of Office Act. His enemies could have asked for nothing better, and they decided to ambush him.

The Radicals wanted to do something never before or since accomplished in American history. They wanted to impeach and convict the President, sending him home in disgrace. The difficulties were great, for they had no real grounds upon which to try the accused. Then, in 1868, Johnson dismissed Secretary of War Stanton. The House of Representatives voted to impeach the President, using his alleged violation of the Tenure of Office Act as the basis of the charges. By March, the American people witnessed the spectacle of their President on trial for his political life.

After weeks of testimony and acrimonious debate, the Senate, acting as a court, voted upon three of the 11 charges against Johnson. None of the 11, except perhaps violation of the Tenure of Office Act, had any substance, and even that one certainly did not approach anything resembling treason, bribery, or a high crime. There were 54 men in the Senate, and two-thirds had to vote against Johnson to convict him. If he could muster 19 votes, he was safe. He managed exactly that number on each of the ballots. By a single vote, the Radicals failed in their unprecedented attempt to destroy a political enemy. As it was, they made history, however unsavory. No Congress since has come close to

The great rush at the left is for the galleries of the Senate to hear Thaddeus Stevens deliver the impeachment message on February 25, 1868. The ticket is for Johnson's friends—and enemies—who wanted to see the impeachment proceedings.

matching the audacity of that move.

The very closeness of the impeachment-trial vote indicated the extent of the Republican power in Congress. A few days after Johnson's narrow escape, his enemies moved off to Chicago for the Republican national convention. There they nominated Ulysses S. Grant, hero of Appomattox and professional soldier, as their Presidential candidate. Schuyler Colfax, Speaker of the House and thoroughgoing Radical, was named as his running mate. It was regarded as an unbeatable team, a supposition that was wholly correct. Here were men who would work with the Radicals men who would help insure the victory over the South and the permanency of the Grand Old Party.

Late in June, Congress again turned to the matter of the South. Back in 1866, Tennessee had been readmitted, and early in June, 1868, Arkansas was also. During that same month, North Carolina, South Carolina, Louisiana, Georgia, Alabama, and Florida were found to be pure enough for membership. Each of these states had to approve the Fourteenth Amendment. All of them except Georgia satisfactorily fulfilled their requirements, and by July they were again represented in Congress. In 1870, Mississippi, Texas, and Virginia returned. Now 10 of the 11 Confederate states were "reconstructed." Only Georgia remained outside the Union, still struggling with the strictures laid down by unbending Northerners in Congress. By 1871, the state was pronounced "tamed," and its Senators were at last seated.

Meanwhile, the Union's foremost war hero was elevated to the Presidency. Grant's election was a simple operation. His name was familiar in every household; when the grizzled, taciturn veteran said, "Let us have peace," the nation reacted favorably. Against such a powerful attraction, the Democratic candidate, Horatio Seymour, had little chance. He and his party were still tainted by their sympathies toward the South.

During Grant's first term, the nation was reconstructed in a narrow political sense. All the errant states resumed their former places, and each was represented in Congress. But there the comparison with prewar days ended. Northern "carpetbaggers" swarmed over the South, occupying key offices and controlling the political apparatus. They were aided by Southern "scalawags," another group of opportunists motivated by desires for personal gain.

With the Thirteenth, Fourteenth, and Fifteenth Amendments rammed down Southern throats, a large black population was enfranchised. The carpetbaggers, backed up by army bayonets, saw to it that these newcomers to suffrage voted the right way. Buying and selling votes became a common practice. Before long, the Southern political scene was one of chaos.

It is wholly understandable that Southerners reacted violently against the work of reconstruction architects in Washington. Under the carpetbag governments, state after state went bankrupt, corruption rose to heights that opened the eyes of the most hardened Americans, and the newly enfranchised blacks, along with their white sponsors, kept social relationships in an uproar. The black, a mere pawn in the game, became the object of Southern hatred, and it was upon him that retribution fell.

As early as 1866, an organization known as the Ku Klux Klan appeared in Tennessee. Its purpose was to control blacks, and consequently his carpetbagger sponsors, through terrorism. Hooded and robed night riders paid calls upon the black electorate, and by means of tricks and threats, frightened the ignorant and suspicious blacks. When threats failed, violence was used. As with all such informal organizations, membership was not highly selective. The original intent of the Klan was largely forgotten, and beating, maiming, and murder were often used to settle personal disputes. This brought action from the government. In 1871, Congress passed severe anti-Klan legislation, and mass arrests followed. The measures were so effective that the Klan was almost eliminated that very year.

The progress of reconstruction was a source of increasingly strong complaint from Southerners. This only convinced many a vindictive Northerner that the correct medicine was being prescribed. While the South writhed in its agonies, the rest of the

CULVER PICTURES

PUCK WANTS "A STRONG MAN AT THE HEAD OF GOVERNMENT" --BUT NOT THIS KIND.

This cartoon indicates that Ulysses S. Grant was a strong President, but implies that all his strength went into supporting his corrupt followers in government positions. The two figures at the right are William W. Belknap, the Secretary of War, who was accused of taking bribes for the sale of trading posts in Indian territory; and O.E. Babcock, Grant's private secretary, who was indicted for defrauding the Internal Revenue department.

707

nation embarked upon a postwar boom, marred only by a slight recession in 1866. For the next decade, inflation and expansion were the economic bywords. Thriving industries worked to supply goods for a growing population and to catch up on the wartime lag in civilian production.

Grant was re-elected in 1872, despite a brief rebellion among Republican liberals. Some of the voters agreed that too much corruption accompanied the economic resurgence, and they voted for the Liberal Democrat, Horace Greeley, but in the main the electorate preferred to let the general have another term. It was hard for Northerners to vote against good times and a thoroughly subjugated South. For such benefits they could afford to put up with considerable corruption. Or so they imagined.

By 1876, times had changed. The war was more than a decade past and much of the Northern bitterness had subsided. Conditions in the South were such that many a Yankee was ready to relent and say that the vanquished had had enough. In the North, the financial panic of 1873 deeply disturbed the business world, causing a good deal of critical comment about government policies. During these times, corruption had surged so high in official circles that the Presidential family itself was touched.

Warning flags popped up in 1874, when in the mid-term election 23 states went Democratic. Two years later, as America's 100th birthday approached and centennial planners made ready to celebrate, voters became thoughtful. Was this the America that the Founding Fathers had envisaged? Was the theory of democracy working as well as they had hoped? Such questions must have caused thinking men to squirm as they looked at the state of public morals.

After failing for nearly 20 years to elect a candidate, the Democrats touched a sensitive political nerve by nominating a recognized reformer, Samuel J. Tilden, governor of New York. The Republicans chose Rutherford B. Hayes of Ohio, largely as a result of the battle between the Grant bitter-enders and the supporters of James G. Blaine. Hayes was a compromise candidate.

The Democrats proved that reform was a popular campaign issue when their candidate polled more popular votes than his opponent in the election. But those in office were determined to stay there, even if it resulted in a national scandal. Resolutely they set about upsetting the will of the electorate.

Seizing upon charges of fraud and violence in Louisiana, Florida, and South Carolina, Republican campaign managers challenged the election. They also questioned one of the electoral votes from Oregon. To squabble over a single vote might appear petty, but in this case it was vital. Tilden had 184 votes in the electoral college. Just one of the disputed votes would put him in office. The Republicans, on the other hand, had to have all of them.

The issue was decided by a commission of 15—five Senators, five Representatives, and five Supreme Court justices. That group divided, seven to seven, leaving in the hands of a single man the decision that would determine a President of the United States. Judge Joseph P. Bradley, a Republican, cast the deciding vote, and in all cases the answer was the same—eight to seven in favor of Hayes. It is small wonder that 19th-century "men of '76," especially the disappointed Democrats, may have thought in revolutionary terms. To them it appeared that the democratic process had failed, as indeed it had. At the time, many did not know that the outcome was determined by a deal whereby Southern Democratic leaders agreed to the Hayes victory, provided federal troops

The corruption of the carpetbaggers and Grant's violent bayonet rule of the South is attacked in this anti-Republican cartoon that was drawn around 1877.

CULVER PICTURES

were withdrawn from the South and at least one Southerner was appointed to the Cabinet. Such knowledge would have done little to strengthen the common man's belief in his political system.

Hayes realized the narrowness of his victory. He knew the temper of the opposition party, not to mention the frustration of the typical Southerner. The country at large was edgy and nervous, and the new President proceeded carefully. One of his first acts was to recall the last army units from the South. They supported the remaining carpetbag governments and without them the whole false structure collapsed. This is precisely what the Southerners had foreseen, and it was why they had been willing to submit to the compromise that made Hayes President. With this single act, a new political power was created—the "solid South." For the remainder of the century, and well into the next, the Democratic Party was able to rely upon its unfailing support.

The immediate result of relaxing the military grip upon the South was, for all practical purposes, to end reconstruction. Emotional scars would remain for a long time and there would be a lingering bitterness, but once again Southerners had control of the political machinery, and they made the most of their situation.

In retrospect, it is clear that reconstruction was a many-sided failure. It failed politically in that Republican efforts to control the South, through the three amendments to the Constitution, did not produce the desired results. It was one thing to gain black suffrage by threat and force; it was something else to get the black voter to the polls in the South. Local laws and terror tactics kept thousands away. The result was bitterness by Southern whites and a deep hatred for the Republican Party. Only bayonets could preserve Republican control, and that situation had to come to an end sometime in a country that stood before the world as a democracy.

Reconstruction was a social failure as well. Radical Republicans imagined they could legislate blacks into a condition of equality, as if by waving a magic wand. There is no question that the former slave had every right to such a reward, but he was far from ready to receive it at that time. Worse, with Northern whites forcing the issue and Southern whites resisting it, the unfortunate black was ground between the upper and lower millstones of political power. When Southerners discriminated against blacks, it was not only an attempt to control him, but at the same time to strike out at the freedman's Northern sponsors. Many a black, who long had enjoyed the care and affection of his white master and other whites, now became the subject of racial discrimination. And his torment came from no action of his own.

Attempts at economic reconstruction also failed for blacks. In most

BETTMAN ARCHIVE

The lot of the black did not greatly improve after the war. He had to go back to raising cotton, this time as a hired field hand or a sharecropper.

cases he merely moved from slavery to a kind of peonage known as sharecropping. As a tenant farmer, he was dependent upon a landlord, and he found it almost as hard to escape from the new slavery as from the old. There was not much the Radicals could do about this situation, except confiscate Southern land and distribute it among blacks. This was not done, although there was talk of it. In the early postwar period, many a black thought he was going to be awarded "40 acres and a mule," as he put it. When the "promised land" did not materialize, the black hired out as a field hand or became a share cropper, and went back to raising cotton. He had legal freedom, but neither economic nor social freedom.

Thus the postwar decade, often referred to as the reconstruction period, was a time of trial for the South and for the very forces of democracy itself across the country. The nation was not reconstructed or restored to what it had been. Instead, the war-torn South was held in a state of subjection as the North grew and prospered. In many ways, the political retribution that followed the war left deeper scars than those caused by shot or shell. The crop the Radicals sowed was hatred, and it grew well in the hothouse climate the Republican Party provided for it.

MAIN TEXT CONTINUES IN VOLUME 9

MUSEUM OF FINE ARTS, BOSTON

In Civil War slang, an "old soldier" was one who was able to devise ways to escape work or to avoid doing special duty. One of the many ways—some of which still exist in today's army—was to feign an illness that would put him in the hospital or on sick leave. Winslow Homer's painting entitled Playing Old Soldier shows a private who is, despite his unhappy face, not sick at all. Presumably the doctor and his orderly have seen enough of such malingerers to make and record a realistic diagnosis.

"Hayfoot, Strawfoot!"

A SPECIAL CONTRIBUTION BY
BRUCE CATTON

The Civil War soldier did what came naturally and usually lacked adequate military training. He was basically a civilian in arms and had much in common with today's G. I.

The volunteer soldier in the American Civil War used a clumsy muzzle-loading rifle, lived chiefly on salt pork and hardtack, and retained to the very end a loose-jointed, informal attitude toward the army. But despite the surface differences, he was blood brother to the G.I. Joe of modern days.

Which is to say that he was basically a civilian in arms. His attitude toward discipline, his officers, and the whole spit-and-polish concept of military existence was essentially one of careless tolerance.

What really set the Civil War soldier apart was the fact that he came from a less sophisticated society. The America of the 1860s was still essentially a rural nation; people lived largely on farms or in country towns and had a hayseed-in-the-hair flavor. For example, every war finds some ardent but underage youngsters who want to enlist. Such a lad today simply swears he is 18 and signs up. The lad of the 1860s felt that to lie to his own government was just plain wrong. So he would scribble the number 18 on a bit of paper and put it inside his shoe. Then, when the recruiting officer asked his age, he could look him straight in the eye and truthfully say, "I am over 18."

The drill sergeants repeatedly found that among the raw recruits there were men so abysmally untaught that they did not know left from right. To teach them how to march, the sergeants would tie a wisp of hay to the left foot and a wisp of straw to the right; then, giving the command to march, they would chant "Hayfoot, strawfoot! Hayfoot, strawfoot!" until everybody had caught on. A common name for a green recruit in those days was "strawfoot."

On the drill field, the men were likely to intone a little rhythmic chant—thus:

March! March! March, old soldier, march!
Hayfoot, strawfoot,
Belly full of bean soup—
March, old soldier, march!

Because of his unsophistication, the Civil War recruit usually joined up with romantic ideas about soldiering. He thought army life was going to be fun. And right at the start, it did have an almost idyllic quality. An Illinois recruit confessed, "It is fun to lie around, face unwashed, hair uncombed, shirt unbuttoned, and everything un-everthinged. It sure beats clerking." Another Illinois boy said, "I don't see why people will stay at home when they can get to soldiering. A year of it is worth getting shot for to any man." The chief worry, in training camp, was that the war would be over before the ardent young recruits could get into it. There was a regiment recruited in northern Pennsylvania in 1861—the 13th Pennsylvania Reserves, known as the Bucktails because the rookies decorated their caps with strips of deer hide. These youthful soldiers, ordered to rendezvous at Harrisburg, marched to the north branch of the Susquehanna, where they built rafts and floated down the river, singing, firing their muskets, and having a gay old time, camping out along the bank at night. Finally they got to Harrisburg, and they served through the worst of the war. They lost most of their men, but they never forgot those first days of army life, when they drifted down a river with a song in the air and the bright lights of adventure shining just ahead.

Discipline in those early regiments was pretty sketchy. Most of them were recruited locally, and everybody more or less knew everybody else. Therefore, the privates knew their officers—whom they usually had

LIBRARY OF CONGRESS

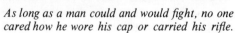

As long as a man could and would fight, no one cared how he wore his cap or carried his rifle.

METROPOLITAN MUSEUM OF ART

elected—so they never saw any need to be formal with them. Within reasonable limits, the Civil War private was willing to do what his company commander told him, but he saw little point in carrying it to extremes.

An Indiana soldier wrote, "We had enlisted to put down the Rebellion, and had no patience with the red-tape tomfoolery of the regular service. The boys recognized no superiors, except in the line of legitimate duty. Shoulder straps waived, a private was ready at the drop of a hat to thrash his commander—a thing that occurred more than once." A New York regiment, drilling on a hot parade ground, heard a private call to his company commander, "Say, Tom, let's quit this darn foolin' around and go over to the sutler's and get a drink." If an officer got complete obedience, he got it because the men recognized him as a natural leader and not because he had a commission.

The Civil War soldier's first loyalty was usually to his regiment, and odd rivalries developed. Outside Washington, a Manhattan regiment was camped near a regiment from Brooklyn. Neither had a chaplain, and one day a minister came to the Manhattan colonel and volunteered to hold religious services for his men. The colonel said his men were rather irreligious, not to say godless, and he feared they would not give the reverend a respectful hearing. The minister replied that he had just held services with the Brooklyn regiment, and the men there had seemed very devout. That was enough for the colonel. He ordered his men paraded for divine worship, and announced that anyone who talked, laughed, or even coughed would be court martialed.

So the clergyman held the services, and everyone was attentive. At the end of his sermon, the minister asked if any man wanted to make public profession of faith; in the Brooklyn regiment, he said, 14 men had. Instantly the New York colonel bellowed, "We're not going to let that Brooklyn regiment beat us at anything! Detail 20 men and have them baptized at once!"

The 48th New York was said to have an unusually large number of ministers serving

714

The group huddled around the fire in this Winslow Homer painting is probably preparing its own food. In the Civil War anyone became the cook who was assigned to the job.

as combat soldiers. The 48th, fairly early in the war, found itself posted in a South Carolina swamp, toiling in semitropical heat. All hands became excessively profane, including the onetime clergymen. A visiting general asked the regiment's lieutenant colonel if he himself was a minister in private life.

"Well, no, General," said the officer apologetically. "I can't say that I was a regularly ordained minister. I was just one of these —— —— local preachers."

Another story was hung on this same 48th New York. A Confederate ironclad gunboat was ready to steam through the swamp and attack the 48th's outposts, and elaborate plans were made to trap it. But it occurred to the colonel that the soldiers could not get into it; it was sheathed in iron, and all its ports would be closed. Remembering that many of his men had come from the less savory districts of New York City, he paraded the regiment and (according to legend) announced, "Now, men, you've been in this cursed swamp for two weeks—up to your ears in mud, no fun, no glory, and blessed poor pay. Here's a chance. Let every man who has had experience as a cracksman or a safeblower step to the front." To the last man, the regiment marched forward four paces and came to attention.

Not unlike this was the reputation of the 6th New York, which included so many Bowery toughs that the rest of the army said a man had to be able to show he had done time in prison in order to get in. The regiment was about to leave for the South, and the colonel gave his men an inspirational talk. They were going, he said, to a land of wealthy plantation owners, where each Southerner had riches of which he could be despoiled. He took out his own gold watch and held it up for all to see, remarking that any deserving soldier could easily get one like it, once he got down to plantation-land. Half an hour later, wanting to know the time, the colonel felt for his watch. It was gone.

If the Civil War army spun lighthearted tales about itself, it had to face a reality that was singularly unpleasant. One of the worst aspects had to do with food. From first to last, no men were enlisted as cooks. A company would simply be issued a quantity of provisions—flour, pork, beans, potatoes, and so on —and invited to prepare the stuff as best it could. Half a dozen men would form a mess and take turns cooking, and everybody had to eat what was prepared or go hungry. Later in

715

the war, each company commander would usually detail two men to act as cooks, and if either knew anything about cooking, the company was in luck. One soldier asserted flatly, "A company cook generally knows less about cooking than any other man in the company. Not being able to learn the drill, and too dirty to appear on inspection, he is sent to the cook house to get him out of the ranks." When an army was on the march, the ration issue usually consisted of salt pork, hardtack, and coffee. The hardtack was good enough, if fresh, which was not always the case; with age it usually got infested with weevils, and veterans remarked that it was better to eat it in the dark.

In the Union Army, most of the time, the soldier could supplement his rations (if he had money) by buying extras from the sutler—a civilian merchant licensed to accompany the army, functioning somewhat as the post exchange does nowadays. The sutler charged high prices and specialized in indigestibles like pies and canned lobster, and those who patronized him regularly came down with stomach upsets. The Confederate Army had few sutlers, which helps to explain why the hungry Confederates were so delighted when they could capture a Yankee camp: To seize a sutler's tent meant high living for the captors, and the men in Lee's army were furious when, in the 1864 campaign, they learned Grant had ordered his army to move without sutlers.

If Civil War cooking arrangements were impromptu and imperfect, the same applied to its hospital system. The surgeons usually were good men by the standards of that day, but no one knew anything about germs or about how wounds became infected, and antisepsis in the operating room was unknown also. It is common to read of a surgeon whetting his scalpel on the sole of his shoe just before operating. The hospital attendants and stretcher-bearers

Food had to be found for the Civil War armies, and the means were often not those of peacetime. This wild group is raiding a farm, grabbing up everything that is in sight.

were detailed from the ranks, and the officer usually chose his most worthless men. As a result, the sick or wounded often got atrocious care.

A result of all this—coupled with the fact that many men enlisted without any medical examinations—was that every regiment suffered a constant attrition from illness and disability. On paper, a regiment was supposed to have between 960 and 1,040 men. A veteran regiment that could muster 350 enlisted men present for duty was considered pretty solid. About twice as many Civil War soldiers died of disease—typhoid, dysentery, and pneumonia were the great killers—as died in action, and besides those who died, many more got medical discharges.

In its wisdom, the Union set up a number of base hospitals in Northern states, far from the battle fronts, on the theory that a man recovering from wounds or sickness would recuperate better back home. Unfortunately, these hospitals were under local control, and the men in them were no longer under the orders of their own regiments or armies. So thousands of men who were sent north for convalescence never returned to fight. Many were detailed for light work in the hospitals, and there they stayed because nobody had the authority to send them back to duty. Others, recovering their health, simply went home. They were answerable to the hospital authorities, not to the army command, and the hospital rarely cared much where they were. The whole system was ideally designed to make desertion easy.

Moreover, many men had little understanding of military discipline. A homesick boy often saw nothing wrong in going home to see the folks. A man from the farm might slip off to put in a crop. Both meant to return but would postpone it from week to week and perhaps end as deserters. This merely reflected the loose discipline and the underlying civilian-mindedness of the rank-and-file soldier. The behavior of Northern armies in Southern territory reflected the same thing— and had a profound effect on the institution of slavery.

Armies of occupation always bear down hard on civilian property. Northern armies

CONFEDERATE MUSEUM

News from home was vital to these Southern soldiers, as it has always been to men at the front.

bore down with especial fervor. Chickens, hams, corn—anything edible that might be found on a plantation—looked like fair game. The typical Northern soldier had strong feelings about the evils of secession. To him the Southerners, being rebels, had forfeited their rights; if evil things happened to them, that was no more than just retribution.

William Tecumseh Sherman is thought of as the archetype of the Northern soldier who believed in pillage and looting, yet during the first years of the war, he resorted to ferocious punishments to keep his men from despoiling Southern property. He even had looters tied up by the thumbs, and all to little effect. Long before he started to commandeer or destroy property as a war measure, his soldiers were practicing it against his will. It was common for a Union colonel to point to a nearby farm and say, "Now, boys, that barn is full of nice fat pigs and chickens. I don't want to see any of you take any of them," whereupon he would look sternly in the opposite direction.

One colonel, punishing some men who had robbed a chicken house, said angrily, "Boys, I want you to understand that I am not punishing you for stealing but for getting caught at it."

Many a family saw the foodstuffs needed for the winter swept away in an hour by grinning hoodlums who could not use a quarter of what they took. Among the foragers there were many lawless characters who took watches and jewels; men would take a piano apart and use the wires to hang pots and pans over the campfire. The Civil War was romantic only at a considerable distance.

The Union soldiers also came to believe that to destroy Southern property was to help win the war. It is at this point that the institution of human slavery enters the picture.

Most Northern soldiers had little feeling against slavery, and little sympathy for the black himself. They were fighting to save the Union, not to end slavery. Nevertheless, they moved effectively to destroy slavery, because they were operating against Southern property and the most easily removable property was the slave. To help the slaves escape was to weaken Southern productive capacity, which in turn weakened Confederate armies. Hence the Union soldier took the "peculiar institution" apart, chattel by chattel, and thus weakened it fatally long before the war ended.

Chiefly, of course, the business of the Civil War soldier was to fight. He fought with weapons that look crude to modern eyes, and he moved by an outmoded system of tactics. The standard infantry weapon in the Civil War was the rifled Springfield—a muzzle-loader firing a conical lead bullet, usually of .54 caliber.

Loading was laborious, and only a good man got off more than two shots a minute. The weapon had a range of nearly a mile, and its "effective range"—that is, the range at which it would hit often enough to make infantry fire truly effective—was about 250 yards. Compared with a modern Garand, the old muzzle-loader is a museum piece; but compared with the weapons on which infantry tactics in the 1860s were based, it was fearfully destructive and efficient. The infantry still moved and fought in the formations of the days of smoothbore muskets, whose effective range was no more than 100 yards and which were wildly inaccurate at any distance.

Armies using those weapons attacked in solid mass formations, the men standing elbow to elbow. They could quickly get from ef-fective range to hand-to-hand fighting, and if they had the right numerical advantage over the defensive line, they could come to grips without losing too many men. But in the Civil War, men would be hit while the rival lines were still half a mile apart, and to advance in mass was to invite wholesale destruction. Tactics had not yet been adjusted to the new rifles; thus attacks could be fearfully costly. And when the defenders dug entrenchments and got some protection, as they fast learned to do, a direct frontal assault could be hardly more than mass suicide. It took the high command a long time to revise their tactics, and battles ran up dreadful casualty lists. For an army to lose 25% of its numbers in a major battle was not uncommon, and in some fights—the Confederate Army at Gettysburg is an outstanding example—the percentage of loss ran close to one-third. Individual units were sometimes nearly wiped out. Some of the Union and Confederate regiments that fought at Gettysburg lost up to 80% of their numbers.

The point is that the discipline that took the Civil War soldier into action, although it was sketchy by modern standards, was nevertheless highly effective in battle. Any armies that could go through such battles as Antietam, Stone's River, Franklin, or Chickamauga and come back for more had little to learn about the business of fighting.

Perhaps the Confederate General D. H. Hill said it once and for all. At the Battle of Malvern Hill, George B. McClellan's men fought a rear-guard action—a bitter, confused fight that came at the end of a solid week of wearing, costly battles and forced marches. Federal artillery wrecked the Confederate assault columns, and as Hill looked out over the battlefield, strewn with dead and wounded boys, he reflected upon the valor of the two armies. He never forgot this, and looking back on it, long after the war was over, he declared in substance, "Give me Confederate infantry and Yankee artillery and I'll whip the world!"

Bruce Catton was Senior Editor of American Heritage Magazine. *He won the Pulitzer Prize for* A Stillness at Appomatox *and wrote many other books about the Civil War.*

Volume 8
ENCYCLOPEDIC SECTION

The two-page reference guide below lists the entries by categories. The entries in this section supplement the subject matter covered in the text of this volume. A **cross-reference** (*see*) means that a separate entry appears elsewhere in this section. However, certain important persons and events mentioned here have individual entries in the Encyclopedic Section of another volume. Consult the Index in Volume 18.

CIVIL RIGHTS

Civil Rights Act of 1866
Emancipation Proclamation
Fifteenth Amendment
Fourteenth Amendment

Ku Klux Klan
Negro troops
Reconstruction Acts
Thirteenth Amendment

CIVIL WAR

Andersonville
Jay Cooke
Copperheads
Pauline Cushman
draft riots
Barbara Fritchie

Gettysburg Address
Merrimack
Battle of the *Monitor* and *Merrimack*
Northwest Conspiracy
Pickett's Charge
Trent Affair

CONFEDERATE MILITARY LEADERS

Turner Ashby
Braxton Bragg
Simon Bolivar Buckner
Jubal A. Early
Richard Ewell
Nathan Forrest
Wade Hampton
William J. Hardee
A. P. Hill
D. H. Hill
John Bell Hood

Stonewall Jackson
Albert Sidney Johnson
Joseph E. Johnston
Robert E. Lee
James Longstreet
John Hunt Morgan
John Singleton Mosby
George Pickett
William Clarke Quantrill
Jeb Stuart
Joseph Wheeler

INVENTORS

John Adolphus Dahlgren

James B. Eads
John Ericsson

THE PRESIDENCY

John Wilkes Booth
Ulysses S. Grant
Rutherford B. Hayes

Andrew Johnson
Abraham Lincoln
Tenure of Office Act
Whiskey Ring

STATESMEN AND POLITICIANS

Nathaniel P. Banks
Judah P. Benjamin
Joseph P. Bradley
Ambrose Burnside
Benjamin F. Butler
Zachariah Chandler
Schuyler Colfax
Jefferson Davis
Hamilton Fish
Ulysses S. Grant
Hannibal Hamlin
Rutherford B. Hayes
Andrew Johnson

Joseph E. Johnston
Abraham Lincoln
James Longstreet
George B. McClellan
John Singleton Mosby
William S. Rosecrans
Edwin Stanton
Thaddeus Stevens
Samuel J. Tilden
Clement Vallandigham
Benjamin Franklin Wade
Joseph Wheeler
Fernando Wood

THOUGHT AND CULTURE

Battle Hymn of the Republic
Mathew B. Brady

D. H. Hill
Julia Ward Howe

UNION MILITARY LEADERS

Orville E. Babcock
Nathaniel P. Banks
Kady Brownell
Don Carlos Buell
Ambrose Burnside
Benjamin F. Butler
John Adolphus Dahlgren
David G. Farragut
Andrew Foote
Ulysses S. Grant
Benjamin Henry Grierson
Henry Halleck

Winfield Scott Hancock
Joseph Hooker
George B. McClellan
George Gordon Meade
John Pope
David Dixon Porter
Fitz-John Porter
William S. Rosecrans
Philip Sheridan
William T. Sherman
George Thomas
Henry Walke
John A. Winslow

A

ANDERSONVILLE. The largest and most notorious of the Confederate military prisons, Andersonville was established in Sumter County, Georgia, as a "stockade for Union enlisted men." It was hurriedly constructed in November, 1863, because of the large number of captured federal soldiers already in Confederate prisons in Richmond, Virginia, and the vast amount of food that was needed to feed them. The camp consisted of a 27-acre log stockade that contained a hospital but no barracks. The first prisoners arrived in February, 1864. During its 13 months of operation, Andersonville held a total of 49,485 prisoners. Of that number, more than one-fourth died. The appalling death rate was due largely to overcrowding. Built to accommodate 10,000 men, Andersonville swelled with a population of 33,006 in the spring of 1864. This resulted in a shortage of food and medicine, lack of housing and cooking facilities, and unsanitary conditions. Starvation, exposure, and such diseases as diarrhea and scurvy drove the death rate so high that a medical commission appointed by the Confederate War Department investigated Andersonville in the spring of 1864. Its recommendation that the majority of captives be moved to other prisons in Georgia and South Carolina was acted upon, and by October, 1864, only about 4,000 men remained within the stockade. After the war, the cruel Swiss prison superintendent, Captain Henry Wirz (?–1865), was convicted by a United States military court of charges of murder and mismanagement and was hanged. The prison graveyard, now a national cemetery,

LIBRARY OF CONGRESS

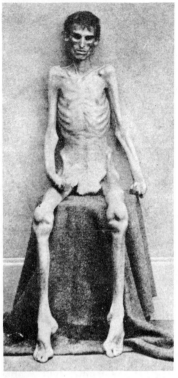

Thousands starved to death at the Confederate prison camp at Andersonville.

contains more than 13,700 Union graves. Libby Prison in Richmond, where only Union officers were held, was almost as notorious as Andersonville. Established in July, 1861, it consisted of eight rooms, 100 feet by 45 feet, in a three-story tobacco warehouse. Nearly 1,200 Northern officers were crowded together in that space at one time (*see p. 670*). Conditions were not much better in Union prisons. Camp Douglas, situated near southern Chicago, held 30,000 Confederate captives during its nearly four years of operation. Within the gates of Elmira Prison, near Elmira, New York, approximately one out of every four of the more than 10,000 Confederate prisoners died. This 30-acre prison camp for enlisted men was closed

in August, 1865, after 13 months of operation.

ASHBY, Turner (1828–1862). A prosperous Virginia planter, Ashby organized a volunteer company of cavalry when John Brown invaded Virginia and raided Harpers Ferry in 1859. When the Civil War broke out, he joined forces with the cavalry of General **Jeb Stuart** (*see*) and helped General **Joseph E. Johnston** (*see*) withdraw from Winchester to Manassas in Virginia. In May and June of 1862, Ashby commanded the horse soldiers of General **Stonewall Jackson** (*see*) in the Shenandoah Valley. On June 6, 1862, during Jackson's retreat, Ashby was killed while fighting a rearguard action.

B

BABCOCK, Orville E. (1835–1884). A distinguished Union officer during the Civil War, Babcock served as private secretary to President **Ulysses S. Grant** (*see*) from 1869 to 1877. He was accused of being involved in one of the major scandals of Grant's second administration, a conspiracy known as the **Whiskey Ring** (*see*), which defrauded the Internal Revenue Department of more than $3,000,000 in liquor taxes. A native of Vermont, Babcock graduated from West Point in 1861 and that summer helped build the defense system around Washington, D.C. He later took part in several campaigns, and he served as chief engineer of the Central District of Kentucky (April–June, 1863) and of the Department of Ohio (January–March, 1864). Babcock subsequently became Grant's aide-de-camp and participated in the Battles of the Wilderness, Spotsylvania, and Cold Harbor and in the siege of Petersburg. His duties included carrying orders and advice, gathering information, and surveying positions. Babcock was promoted to brigadier general in 1865. He remained Grant's aide until Grant became President in 1869, at which time he accompanied him to the White House as his secretary. In December, 1875, Babcock was indicted by a St. Louis grand jury "for conspiracy to defraud the revenue," but was acquitted the following February after Grant sent a supporting statement in his defense to the court. Babcock subsequently resigned his post and worked as an engineer.

BANKS, Nathaniel Prentiss (1816–1894). Banks was a prominent Massachusetts-born politician who served as a Union general in the Civil War. As a youth, Banks worked in a local cotton mill, a job that won him the nickname Bobbin Boy of Massachusetts. He soon became active in local politics and was elected to the state legislature (1849–1852). He then served (1853–1857) in the House of Representatives, switching allegiance from the Democratic Party to the Know-Nothing Party in 1855. Although he was a Know-Nothing in 1856, his election as Speaker of the House that year with strong Republican support on the 133rd ballot was hailed as that party's first national victory. Banks himself subsequently became a Republican. He resigned from Congress when he was elected governor of Massachusetts (1858–1861). Banks was president of the Illinois Central Railroad when the Civil War started. He was commissioned a major general of volunteers in the Union Army. During the Shenandoah campaign in 1862, Banks' out-

numbered forces were defeated three times by **Stonewall Jackson** (*see*) in the Battles of Front Royal, Winchester, and Cedar Mountain, all in Virginia. Banks commanded the military district of Washington, D.C., in the fall of 1862, and he was then given command of the Department of New Orleans. Banks helped **Ulysses S. Grant** (*see*) open the Mississippi River to navigation by attacking Port Hudson, Louisiana, which surrendered in July, 1863. The next year, he took part in the Red River expedition to Texas, but he was unsuccessful in dislodging Southern forces blocking his way in Louisiana. He resigned from the army shortly after the end of the war and represented Massachusetts in the House (1865–1873, 1875–1879, and 1889–1891).

***BATTLE HYMN OF THE REPUBLIC.* See Howe, Julia Ward.**

BELKNAP, William Worth (1829–1890). Belknap's good reputation as a Union commander was offset by his dishonesty as Secretary of War in the 1870s. Belknap was admitted to the bar in 1851 and began practicing law in Iowa, where he was a state legislator (1857–1858) before joining the 15th Iowa Infantry at the outset of the Civil War. Commending his leadership at the Battle of Shiloh, Tennessee, in April, 1862, a superior officer reported, "Major Belknap was always in the right place at the right time, directing and encouraging officers and men as coolly as a veteran." Belknap later served at the siege of Vicksburg in 1863 and commanded a division under General **William T. Sherman** (*see*) during the invasion of Georgia and the Carolinas the following year. In 1869, President **Ulysses S. Grant** (*see*) appointed

Belknap his Secretary of War. Seven years later, a Congressional committee discovered that he had received a total of $24,450 in bribes for appointing John S. Evans as post trader at Fort Sill, Oklahoma. The House of Representatives voted unanimously to impeach Belknap, who then resigned. When subsequently tried by the Senate, according to constitutional procedure, Belknap was found guilty by a vote of 35 to 25. However, the margin was short of the necessary two-thirds for conviction, which would have formally removed him from office and disqualified him from holding any further federal posts. Most of the 25 Senators who voted against Belknap's conviction believed that his resignation had taken the case out of the Senate's jurisdiction. Belknap later practiced law in Washington, D.C., until his death.

BENJAMIN, Judah Philip (1811–1884). Called "the brains of the Confederacy," Benjamin was a key figure in the rebel government. Born in the Virgin Islands, he settled in Louisiana in 1828 and became a successful lawyer and planter. Benjamin was elected to the first of two terms in the Senate in 1852 and was one of the first Southern lawmakers to speak out for secession from the Union. He resigned from the Senate in 1861 to serve in the Confederate cabinet, first as Attorney General, then as Secretary of War, and finally as Secretary of State. A close friend and adviser to **Jefferson Davis** (*see*), Benjamin was blamed, often unfairly, for several Confederate defeats in early 1862, while he was still Secretary of War. Nevertheless, Davis trusted him completely and late in the war supported Benjamin's proposal that slaves who volunteered to fight for the South should be freed afterward. The Confederate Congress voted in 1865 to allow slaves to fight (actually, none ever did), but it did not provide for emancipation. This was a bitter defeat for Benjamin, who was assailed by many Southern leaders. At the war's end, Benjamin escaped to Britain, where he again practiced law. His legal writings and brilliance in the British courts made him one of the leading lawyers of his day. He retired in 1883 after a streetcar accident in Paris and died there a year later.

LIBRARY OF CONGRESS

Four coconspirators of John Wilkes Booth were hanged together on July 7, 1865.

BOOTH, John Wilkes (1838–1865). On the evening of April 14, 1865, at Ford's Theatre in Washington, D.C., Booth shot and mortally wounded President **Abraham Lincoln** (*see*). Born in Maryland, Booth belonged to a family of famous actors. His father, Junius Brutus Booth (1796–1852), and his brothers Edwin Booth (1833–1893) and Junius Brutus Booth, Jr. (1821–1883), were all renowned Shakespearean actors. Booth made his stage debut at the age of 17. Although an erratic and undisciplined performer, he possessed marked dramatic gifts and a striking appearance. However, he abandoned his career to become involved in secret attempts to aid the Confederacy. Although the rest of his family supported the Union, Booth, a defender of slavery, secretly sided with the South. As early as 1864, he conspired with several Southern sympathizers to kidnap or assassinate the President. The plot was foiled when Lincoln did not appear, as scheduled, at a hospital where the conspirators planned to seize him. On April 14, 1865, five days after the Confederate surrender at Appomattox, Booth learned that Lincoln was expected to attend

Ford's Theatre. The assassin entered the Presidential box while a guard was away from his post and shot the President in the back of the head. Leaping onto the stage, he shouted, *"Sic semper tyrannis! The South is avenged!"* He then fled on a waiting horse. At the same time, Secretary of State William H. Seward (1801–1872) was stabbed in bed by another conspirator, but survived. On April 26, Booth was cornered by federal troops in a barn near Bowling Green, Virginia. To flush him out, the barn was set on fire. Although under orders not to shoot, one soldier fired into the barn. When Booth was finally dragged from the barn, he was found wounded. Booth subsequently died of a gunshot wound. It is uncertain whether he shot himself or had been hit by the soldier. In all, eight persons were convicted after a sensational, legally irregular trial at which evidence was suppressed. Four of them were hanged simultaneously on July 7, 1865: Lewis T. Powell (1845?–1865), alias Lewis Paine, who had attacked Seward; David E. Herold (1842?–1865), who had assisted Powell and had later been captured with Booth; George A. Atzerodt (?–1865), who was sup-

posed to have assassinated Vice-President **Andrew Johnson** (*see*), but had backed out at the last minute; and Mrs. Mary E. Surratt (1820–1865), at whose boardinghouse in Washington the conspirators had met to work out the plot. In addition, Dr. Samuel Mudd (1833–1883), a Maryland doctor who had set the leg that Booth apparently broke when he jumped onto the stage at Ford's Theatre, was tried as a conspirator and sentenced to life imprisonment at Fort Jefferson, off Key West, Florida. He was pardoned in 1869, after nursing the garrison there through a yellow-fever epidemic.

BRADLEY, Joseph P. (1813–1892). A Supreme Court Justice and a Republican, Bradley cast the deciding vote in favor of Republican **Rutherford B. Hayes** over his Democratic opponent, **Samuel J. Tilden** (*see both*), in the disputed Presidential election of 1876. Born in upstate New York, Bradley was admitted to the New Jersey bar in 1839 and subsequently developed a respected patent- and corporate-law practice in that state. In February, 1870, President **Ulysses S. Grant** (*see*) appointed him Associate Justice

NATIONAL ARCHIVES

Brady photographed the ruins of the Confederate capital of Richmond in 1865.

of the Supreme Court, where he served for the next 22 years. In the election of 1876, Tilden received the majority of the popular votes, winning by a margin of about 250,000 votes out of the more than 8,000,000 that were cast. The Republican leaders refused to accept the validity of the returns in Louisiana, Florida, South Carolina, and Oregon and managed to invalidate enough Democratic ballots in those states to declare Hayes victorious. The Democrats refused to accept this state of affairs, and on December 6, 1876, two sets of returns were filed from the four disputed states. According to the Constitution, electoral votes are "counted"—that is, validated—by Congress, but the Republican-controlled Senate would have supported Hayes, while the House, where the Democrats had a majority, would have backed Tilden. Therefore, on January 29, 1877, Congress set up an Electoral Commission to break the deadlock. It consisted of five Senators, five Representatives, and five Supreme Court Justices. Of these, seven were Republicans, seven were Democrats, and one was an impartial independent, Justice David Davis (1815–1886). Before the commission could act, Davis was elected a Senator from Illinois and was disqualified. He was replaced on the commission by Bradley. Although he was supposed to be neutral, Bradley was pressured by his party to support the Republican candidate. His deciding vote resulted in the eight-to-seven electoral victory for Hayes, who was declared officially elected on March 2, 1877.

BRADY, Mathew B. (1823?–1896). The most famous American pioneer photographer, Brady was especially noted for his coverage of the Civil War. He also photographed all the Presidents of the United States from John Quincy Adams (1767–1848) to William McKinley (1843–1901), with the exception of William Henry Harrison (1773–1841). Born in upstate New York, Brady learned the daguerreotype process from the artist and inventor Samuel F. B. Morse (1791–1872). This was the earliest practical type of photography. The picture was fixed on a copper plate coated with silver iodide after an exposure of several minutes, during which the subject had to remain absolutely still. The picture was developed by passing across it poisonous mercury fumes. About 1844, Brady opened his own studio in New York City and, using the daguerreotype process, he soon became a leading portrait photographer, winning acclaim, patronage, and awards. In 1850, he published his *Gallery of Illustrious Americans,* and about five years later he discarded the daguerreotype process and adopted the wet-plate method. This process involved the use of glass-plate negatives that could then be used to make several prints on specially treated paper. The exposure time was shorter, but the plates had to be developed immediately. As a result, Brady con-structed a portable darkroom in a covered wagon so he could photograph outdoor scenes. Brady and his assistants used this process to take more than 3,500 photographs of the battles, leaders, troops, and scenes of the Civil War. After the war, Brady found himself heavily in debt and was completely ruined by the Panic of 1873. In 1874, the government bought 2,000 of his Civil War photographs for $3,000, and the rest were sold to collectors. The government collections are kept in the National Archives and the Library of Congress in Washington, D.C. Although Congress voted Brady $25,000 in 1875, he died in poverty and neglect.

BRAGG, Braxton (1817–1876). A Louisiana planter and West Point graduate (1837), Bragg was a Confederate general whose unpopularity and vagueness often led to defeats on the battlefield. At the Battle of Shiloh in April, 1862, Bragg took over the command of General **Albert Sidney Johnston** (*see*) after Johnston was killed, and he lost the battle to General **Ulysses S. Grant** (*see*). Bragg, who had been promoted to full general during the battle, was next put in command of the Army of the Tennessee. In August, 1862, he led an ill-fated invasion of

Kentucky, where the assaults of Union General **Don Carlos Buell** (*see*) forced him to retreat into Tennessee. There he was outmaneuvered by Union General **William S. Rosecrans** (*see*). However, after retreating to Georgia, Bragg defeated Rosecrans at the Battle of Chickamauga, September 19-20, 1863. That same autumn, Bragg laid siege to Union forces at Chattanooga, Tennessee, but was attacked and again routed by Grant. After this defeat, Bragg was forced to give up his command. He became military adviser to Confederate President **Jefferson Davis** (*see*). At the close of the war, Bragg was captured by Northern troops in North Carolina but was soon paroled. He then moved to Texas, where he worked as a civil engineer. During his military career, Bragg was plagued by chronic headaches and ill health, which may have been the causes of his quarrelsome nature. "He was frequently in the saddle when the more appropriate place for him would have been in bed," one of his fellow officers wrote.

BROWNELL, Kady (1842-?). The wife of a Union soldier, Kady took part in two battles during the Civil War. Kady was born in Africa, where her father, a British soldier, was stationed. She married Robert S. Brownell, an American, and at the outbreak of the Civil War was allowed to enlist with her husband in the First Rhode Island Regiment. Kady, who carried a sword, a rifle, and a flag, saw action at the First Battle of Bull Run in July, 1861. When her husband later transferred to the Fifth Rhode Island Regiment, she went with him. During the skirmish in which General **Ambrose Burnside** (*see*) captured New Bern, North Carolina, in March, 1862,

Brownell was wounded, and after recuperating he was discharged from the army. Burnside also gave Kady an honorable discharge and presented her with a sword and the colors.

BUCKNER, Simon Bolivar (1823-1914). A Kentuckian named for the South American revolutionary leader Simon Bolivar (1783-1830), Buckner served as a general in the Confederate Army. He graduated from West Point in 1844 and fought in the Mexican War. He subsequently taught at West Point before resigning from the army in 1855. Three years later, he settled in Louisville, where he recruited and trained a Kentucky militia. Buckner worked hard, but unsuccessfully, to keep his state neutral in the Civil War. However, Unionists in the Kentucky legislature took control of the state's military affairs in 1861, and he joined the Confederacy and was made a brigadier general. In his first engagement, at Fort Donelson, Tennessee, in February, 1862, Buckner was forced to surrender by General **Ulysses S. Grant** (*see*) and was taken prisoner. He returned to the South after a prisoner exchange. With General **Braxton Bragg** (*see*), Buckner led troops into Kentucky in the fall of 1862 and at the Battles of Chattanooga, Tennessee, and Chickamauga, Georgia, a year later. During the last year of the war, he commanded Southern forces in Louisiana. After the Civil War, the terms of surrender denied Buckner the right to return to Kentucky, so he moved to New Orleans and became involved in newspaper work and the insurance business. By 1868, former Confederates had regained control of Kentucky, and Buckner returned to become editor of

the Louisville *Courier*. He was elected governor of the state in 1887. After a four-year term, he retired to his farm but remained a powerful influence in Kentucky politics until his death.

BUELL, Don Carlos (1818-1898). Until the Battle of Perryville, Kentucky, in October, 1862, Buell—a native of Ohio and a graduate of West Point (1841)—was an esteemed Union general. As commander of the Department of the Ohio, he had aided General **Ulysses S. Grant** (*see*) in the attack on Bowling Green, Kentucky, in February, 1862. After the fall of Fort Donelson, Tennessee, that same month, he pursued the Southern forces to Nashville. In April, his troops reached the Battle of Shiloh, Tennessee, in time to drive the Confederates from the field. Then came Perryville. On October 8, 1862, Buell fought a fierce battle with Southern troops commanded by General **Braxton Bragg** (*see*) but failed to press the pursuit of the retreating Confederates. He was forced to give up his command and had to wait for more than a year, while an inquiry was held, for the federal government to give him another. In 1864, Buell was discharged as a major general of volunteers, and he promptly resigned his commission. Grant recommended that he be accepted into the army again, but no action was taken. Buell settled in Kentucky in the postwar years and became the head of a mining company.

BURNSIDE, Ambrose Everett (1824-1881). A reluctant commander, Burnside was dropped from the Union Army after an ill-fated charge at Petersburg, Virginia, in which about 4,000 of

NATIONAL ARCHIVES

Ambrose Burnside

his men were lost. Born in Indiana, Burnside graduated from West Point in 1847, and after brief service in the Mexican War and in fighting Indians he resigned from the army in 1853 to manufacture firearms in Rhode Island. In 1856, he patented a breech-loading rifle. Burnside, who had enlisted as a colonel at the outbreak of the Civil War, was promoted to brigadier general in August, 1861, after the First Battle of Bull Run. Soon afterward, his troops drove Southern forces from the North Carolina coast. After taking part in the Antietam campaign in Maryland in September, 1862, Burnside was named commander of the Army of the Potomac, a post he had twice before declined. That December, at Fredericksburg, Virginia, his troops tried to dislodge a strong

Southern defense and were badly mauled. After the battle, Burnside became involved in a dispute over how to continue the fighting and was replaced by General **Joseph Hooker** (*see*). In March, 1863, Burnside took command of the Department of the Ohio. He succeeded in capturing the Confederate raider **John Hunt Morgan** (*see*) and in laying siege to Knoxville, Tennessee. He returned to the Army of the Potomac as a corps commander under General **George Gordon Meade** (*see*), but in the summer of 1864 at the siege of Petersburg he tried to seize a heavily fortified ridge. Nearly 4,000 of his troops were killed, wounded, or captured. Meade held a court of inquiry, which blamed Burnside for the disaster, and soon afterward he took an extended leave of absence from the army. Burnside was later a railroad executive and was elected governor of Rhode Island three times (1866–1869). He served as a Senator (1875–1881) until his death. A distinguished-looking man, Burnside began the fashion of wearing long side-whiskers, or "burnsides," which are also called, in a reversal of his name, "sideburns."

BUTLER, Benjamin F. (1818–1893). The blunders made by this Union general—called Beast Butler by Southerners—caused several serious problems for President **Abraham Lincoln** (*see*) during the Civil War. At its outset in 1861, Butler was a prominent politician in Massachusetts and a general in the state militia. He was put in command of the Annapolis District. Attempting to keep Maryland in the Union, Butler declared martial law. Lincoln, fearful of how that critical border state would react, removed him

from command. Butler was next put in charge of Fortress Monroe in Virginia. He was the first to apply the term *contraband* to runaway slaves and to confiscate them as enemy property, winning him many friends among radicals in the North but another reprimand from Lincoln. Butler, however, was an influential Democrat, and Lincoln could not afford to remove him from command. He became the military governor of New Orleans in May, 1862. His harsh measures there brought the hostile population under control. Butler's order stating that any woman insulting a Union soldier would be treated as a "woman of the street [prostitute]" aroused indignation throughout the South and in several foreign nations, and Lincoln removed him as governor in December, 1862. Still politically powerful, Butler was then given command of the Army of the James, though he suffered several embarrassing defeats. General **Ulysses S. Grant** (*see*) finally insisted upon his recall early in 1865. After the war, Butler served 10 years (1867–1875 and 1877–1879) in the House of Representatives. As an anti-Southern Radical Republican, he took a leading part in the impeachment proceedings against President **Andrew Johnson** (*see*). Butler was elected governor of Massachusetts in 1882. In 1884, he was the Presidential candidate on the Greenback and Anti-Monopoly tickets, but he failed to receive any electoral votes and retired from political activity.

C

CHANDLER, Zachariah (1813–1879). "Old Zack" was a tough, outspoken Republican who fought hard in Congress against slavery and secession. Chandler left his native New Hampshire and moved to Detroit in 1833, where he became a wealthy realtor and banker. After serving as mayor (1851–1852) of Detroit, he helped organize the Republican Party and became its leader in his own state. Elected to the United States Senate (1857–1875), Chandler became an anti-Southern Radical Republican during the Civil War. A firm believer in dealing harshly with the South, he thought that the Reconstruction policies of President **Abraham Lincoln** and his successor, **Andrew Johnson** (*see both*), were too lax. In 1875, Chandler was named Secretary of the Interior by President **Ulysses S. Grant** (*see*). He reorganized the Department of the Interior and dismissed many of its employees because of dishonesty and incompetence. He died a few months after being elected again to the Senate in 1878.

CIVIL RIGHTS ACT OF 1866. Although the slaves had been freed by the **Emancipation Proclamation** (*see*) in 1863, some Southern states after the Civil War established "Black Codes" to curtail black freedom. These codes limited the legal rights of blacks and were an attempt to force blacks to work for their former masters. Congress answered these restrictive measures with the Civil Rights Act of 1866, which granted citizenship to persons "of every race and color" born in the United States, with the exception of any Indians who were not paying taxes. The act also guaranteed that the federal government would protect the personal and property rights of these newly created citizens within any state or territory. President **Andrew Johnson** (*see*) vetoed

the act, calling it a violation of states' rights, but Congress overrode the veto. Because of questions about the constitutionality of the Civil Rights Act—it contradicted the Supreme Court's ruling in the Dred Scott Case of 1857—the **Fourteenth Amendment** (*see*) was ratified in 1868 to confirm the citizenship of blacks. The Civil Rights Act of 1866 was ruled unconstitutional by the Supreme Court in 1883, but judicial and Congressional actions in the 1950s and 1960s have reaffirmed and supplemented this pioneering, post-Civil War legislation.

COLFAX, Schuyler (1823–1885). Grant's first Vice-President, for whom **Abraham Lincoln** (*see*) once predicted a "bright future," saw his public life cut short by scandal. Born in New York City, Colfax moved with his family to Indiana in 1836, where he became an auditor, a journalist, and subsequently the publisher of a leading Whig Party newspaper, the *St. Joseph Valley Register*. In the 1850s, he helped organize the state's Republican Party. Colfax was elected to the first of eight terms in the House of Representatives in 1855 and became Speaker in 1863. His position as Speaker and his advocacy of black suffrage made Colfax— "a good-tempered, chirping, warbling, real canary bird"—an obvious choice as running mate for **Ulysses S. Grant** (*see*) in 1868. During the Presidential campaign of 1872, in which Colfax's renomination was defeated on the first ballot, the New York *Sun* exploded the Credit Mobilier scandal in which Colfax, among others, was implicated. Colfax was accused of accepting stock in 1868 from the fraudulent Credit Mobilier company in exchange for political protection. Committees of both the House and

the Senate were set up to investigate. Although Colfax declared that he was not guilty, contemporary opinion found "it is impossible to believe that he told the truth." He was not censured by Congress, because his alleged misconduct had occurred before he became Vice-President, but the investigators uncovered a $4,000 bribe he had accepted from a government contractor during the 1868 election. Because of the scandal, Colfax never held public office after leaving the Vice-Presidency in 1873. He spent the remainder of his life lecturing and working for a fraternal organization, the Odd Fellows.

COOKE, Jay (1821–1905). This Philadelphia banker was known as the financier of the Civil War because of the major role he played in raising the money that the Union needed to pay for the costs of the war. As a youth, Cooke worked as a store clerk in his native town—present-day Sandusky,

CULVER PICTURES

Jay Cooke

Ohio—and then as clerk for a canalboat line in Philadelphia. In

1839, he entered a banking house in Philadelphia and launched his career in finance. In 1861, he formed his own banking firm, Jay Cooke & Company, and for 12 years was one of the nation's leading financiers. During the Civil War, Cooke marketed large federal-government loans. Between 1862 and 1864, he persuaded close to 1,000,000 citizens to put up the $500,000,000 that the government borrowed to conduct the war. After the war, Cooke tried to raise $100,000,000 to finance Western railroads, especially the Northern Pacific. He failed and was forced to close his bank, a step that helped bring on the nationwide Panic of 1873. Later in life, Cooke made a new fortune, partly through mining investments in Utah, and managed to pay off the debts from his railroad failure.

COPPERHEADS. *See* **Wood, Fernando.**

CUSHMAN, Pauline (1835–1893). A New Orleans-born actress, Pauline Cushman was a famous Union spy during the Civil War. In the spring of 1863, she managed to get behind the Southern lines to collect military information for the North. Miss Cushman was captured with "compromising papers" near the headquarters of Confederate General **Braxton Bragg** (*see*) at Tullahoma, Tennessee. She was court-martialed and sentenced to be hanged. In the meantime, she was imprisoned at Shelbyville, Tennessee. However, in June, 1863, before the sentence could be carried out, the Confederate troops retreated from Shelbyville, leaving her there. Miss Cushman was able to give the advancing Army of the Cumberland under Union General **William S. Rosecrans** (*see*) valua-

LIBRARY OF CONGRESS

Pauline Cushman

ble information concerning Confederate military strategy, but by this time she was too well-known to continue spying. She returned to the North, where she was acclaimed as "the spy of the Cumberland." Miss Cushman's later life was unhappy, and she committed suicide in San Francisco in 1893. She was given a military-style funeral and buried in a cemetery reserved for members of the Grand Army of the Republic.

D

DAHLGREN, John Adolphus (1809–1870). Dahlgren was the inventor of a naval cannon used extensively by the Union during the Civil War (*see p. 691*). The son of the Swedish consul in Philadelphia, Dahlgren was educated in

a Quaker school and entered the American navy in 1826. While on ordnance duty (1847–1863) in Washington, D.C., Dahlgren reorganized and equipped the entire navy yard, an accomplishment that was of crucial importance to the Union during the Civil War. In 1848, Dahlgren's suggestion for equipping the navy with boat howitzers was approved. Three years later he had completed the design for the Dahlgren gun, which had curved walls to prevent an explosion in the barrel, a common occurrence in other cannons. The guns were nicknamed "soda-water bottles" because of their shape and were used extensively by the navy during the Civil War. In 1862, Dahlgren was appointed chief of the navy's ordnance bureau. However, he wished to see combat duty, and after he was appointed a rear admiral in 1863, he took command of the South Atlantic Blockading Squadron. Dahlgren assisted General **William T. Sherman** (*see*) in the capture of Savannah in 1864. Just before his death, he was placed in charge of the navy yard in Washington.

DAVIS, Jefferson (*Continued from Volume 7*). As provisional President of the Confederacy, Davis faced a formidable task. The South was outnumbered by the North in terms of the men available for military service by a ratio of nearly 4 to 1. It had few arms, few industries, no navy, and no gunpowder mills. In addition, extreme states' rightists in the Confederate Congress resented any demands placed upon their states by the central government. Even though Davis was unanimously elected President in a popular election held in November, 1861, he was continually at odds with

Confederate Congressmen. In February, 1862, at Davis' urging, they grudgingly gave him the power to suspend the writ of habeas corpus, but states' rights sentiments were so strong that, in some instances, government authorities would jail a man who would then be released by state authorities. In April, 1862, Davis demanded and received a conscription bill from his Congress. However, adamant state officials, including the governor of Georgia, Joseph E. Brown (1821–1895), actually encouraged draft evasion. Beset by economic problems, Davis in April, 1863, got the Confederate Congress to enact a sweeping tax bill to finance the war, but some states refused to collect any revenues, and that autumn a majority opposed to Davis was elected to Congress. In November, 1864, Davis urged the Confederate Congress to authorize the purchase of 40,000 slaves for the army. At the end of their service, they were to be set free. Davis hoped the offer of emancipation might still bring Britain and France, which were both opposed to slavery, into the war on the Confederacy's side. After an extended debate, the Confederate Congress passed a law authorizing a conscription of 300,000 men irrespective of their color, but no mention was made of emancipation. Resentment toward Davis increased as Southern forces began to lose battles. Davis always considered himself a military genius and often planned battle strategies, and so some Southerners blamed "the pigheaded perverseness of Davis" for Confederate losses. Throughout the war, Davis maintained his desire for Southern independence. He rejected all peace overtures because none included recognition of an independent South. Advancing Union armies forced Davis to flee from Richmond, Virginia, on April 3, 1865. He fled to Georgia, hoping eventually to leave the country, but he was captured at Irwinville, Georgia, on May 10, 1865. A story, embellished by Northern cartoonists, said that he was disguised in a woman's hoopskirt and was carrying gold when captured. In fact, Davis' wife had thrown her shawl to him, apparently to keep him warm, a few minutes before his capture. Davis was imprisoned at Fort Monroe, Virginia. He was kept in irons at first, but he became so ill that he was unshackled and given comfortable quarters with his family. Davis was never brought to trial, and after two years he was released. To some, he became a scapegoat for the South's defeat. In 1881, he published a defense of his actions, *The Rise and Fall of the Confederate States*. He spent his last years on an estate in Mississippi, refusing to ask the federal government for a pardon. Congress restored his citizenship in 1958, nearly 70 years after his death. Davis is buried in Richmond, Virginia.

DRAFT RIOTS. Opposition to federal military conscription in the North during the Civil War was centered in New York City. The Enrollment Act of March 3, 1863—which made all able-bodied men between 20 and 35 and single men up to 45 eligible for the draft—was denounced as unconstitutional by New York's Governor Horatio Seymour (1810–1886). The poor were especially enraged by the provision of the act that allowed men to buy exemption from service for $300. The drawing of the names of New Yorkers who would be drafted began on July 11, 1863. Two days later, a mob of about 50,000 people, most of them Irish-American laborers, began a four-day rampage of lynching blacks, burning, and looting. Union troops, summoned from the Army of the Potomac near Richmond, were rushed to the city. Before order was restored, more than 1,000 persons had been killed or wounded and nearly

MUSEUM OF THE CITY OF NEW YORK; J. CLARENCE DAVIES COLLECTION

Picket fences were pulled apart to make clubs during the draft riots in New York.

$1,500,000 worth of property had been destroyed. A similar uprising threatened in Boston was suppressed by federal troops. Other disturbances occurred in Vermont, New Hampshire, and Ohio. The draft in New York was resumed in August under guard.

E

EADS, James Buchanan (1820–1887). Eads was the designer of a fleet of steam-driven, ironclad gunboats used by the North during the Civil War. His career as an inventor and self-educated engineer began in 1838, when he signed on a Mississippi steamboat as a "mud clerk." Impressed by the large number of ships wrecked in the river with their cargoes aboard, he built a diving bell out of a 40-gallon whiskey barrel, pat-

MISSOURI HISTORICAL SOCIETY

James B. Eads

ented an improved version of it, and went into the steamboat-salvage business in 1842. Fourteen years later, Eads presented Congress with a practical method of removing the wrecks and natural snags that made river navigation dangerous. Although his proposal

was rejected, it brought him to the attention of President **Abraham Lincoln** (*see*), who called him to Washington in 1861 for advice on the defense of Western rivers. Eads suggested the construction of a fleet of steam-driven gunboats with iron-plated sides to deflect shell fire. Eads contracted to build seven such ships, of 600 tons each, within 65 days. Despite chaotic industrial conditions, he organized 4,000 workmen, who finished the first gunboat, the *St. Louis,* in a month and a half (*see p. 689*). Eads then built 13 other such ships, as well as seven iron-plated transports, or "tin-clads," and four mortar boats. After the war, Eads designed and supervised the construction (1867–1874) of a unique railroad bridge across the Mississippi at St. Louis. Still called Eads Bridge, it was the first steel-arch bridge ever built. Eads next devised a system of jetties to open a permanent channel at the mouth of the Mississippi into the Gulf of Mexico. This achievement, completed in 1879, brought him an international reputation as an engineer.

EARLY, Jubal Anderson (1816–1894). A graduate of West Point (1837) and a veteran of the Mexican War, "Jube" Early was a Confederate general who suffered two major defeats that ended his military career. A Virginian, he fought in several battles in his own state during the Civil War and then raided Union forces throughout the Shenandoah Valley. In July, 1864, he ordered the burning of Chambersburg, Pennsylvania, after the town refused to pay a ransom of $100,000 in gold or $500,000 in paper money. Early's first defeat came after a series of battles with Union troops under General **Philip Sheridan** (*see*). The

decisive clash took place at Cedar Creek, Virginia, on October 19, 1864, after Sheridan made his famous 15-mile ride from Winchester to rally his men. Early's second defeat came on March 2, 1865, when his army was destroyed at Waynesboro, Virginia, by the troops of General George Custer (1839–1876). Early's losses aroused Southern public opinion against him, and he was relieved of his command. After **Robert E. Lee** (*see*) surrendered at Appomattox in April, 1865, Early traveled west in disguise to help Confederate General Edmund Kirby-Smith (1824–1893), but Kirby-Smith surrendered that June. Early then fled the country, first to Mexico and then to Canada. In 1869, he moved to Virginia, where he practiced law. He remained a bitter, outspoken foe of the North until his death.

EMANCIPATION PROCLAMATION. The Emancipation Proclamation, which was issued by President **Abraham Lincoln** (*see*), declared that after January 1, 1863, all slaves in the areas "wherein the people . . . are this day in rebellion . . . are, and hence forward shall be free." Primarily a propaganda measure, the proclamation did not immediately free all the slaves in the United States, nor was that Lincoln's intention. Throughout the Civil War, the preservation of the Union—not the abolition of slavery—was Lincoln's main concern. He always advocated the gradual abolition of slavery, with compensatory payments to the slave owners. In the early stages of the war, he was careful not to alienate border states such as Kentucky and Missouri, which permitted slavery, and he was critical of the emancipation proclamations issued by several Union generals. However, by the summer of 1862 several factors prompted him to prepare an emancipation proclamation. Congress had already prohibited slavery in Washington, D.C., in April, 1862, compensating slave owners for the loss of their "property." That June, slavery was also abolished—this time without compensation—in the territories. Lincoln feared that European nations, especially France and Britain, would recognize the Confederacy unless the Union war aim included a moral cause, namely abolition. Also, citizens in the North were now openly urging a stronger stand against slavery. Accordingly, on July 22, 1862, Lincoln read to his cabinet the draft of a proclamation that he had decided to issue. Secretary of State William H. Seward (1801–1879) persuaded him to wait until after a Union victory to issue it. The defeat of the Confederate forces at the Battle of Antietam in mid-September of that year provided a perfect opportunity, and on September 22, 1862, Lincoln issued a preliminary proclamation. This stated that union, not abolition, was the Northern war aim, and that, although emancipation would follow, slave owners would be repaid for their losses. Lincoln added that the emancipation of slaves in Confederate-controlled areas would go into effect on January 1, 1863. Before that date, Lincoln tried but failed to get Congress to provide compensation to the slaveholders covered by the proclamation. On New Year's Day, 1863, he issued the final Emancipation Proclamation, in which he stated the exact areas—all still in Southern control—where the slaves would be freed. He also said that freed slaves would be accepted into the federal

army. Lincoln totally excluded from the proclamation the freeing of slaves in border states within the Union and in other areas where Union forces were in control. Thus, the proclamation, which he described as a "war measure for suppressing" the rebellious Southern states, did not actually free any slaves. Slavery was not legally and completely abolished until the enactment of the **Thirteenth Amendment** (*see*) in 1865.

ERICSSON, · John (1803–1889). This Swedish-born inventor designed and built the ironclad ship *Monitor* for the Union in the Civil War. Ericsson left Sweden in 1826 and went to England, where he built the *Novelty,* one of the first steam locomotives. He came to the United States in 1839 to build a propeller-driven ship for the United States Navy. The vessel, the *Princeton,* was the first warship with a screw propeller, a device he had invented. During the ship's trials in 1844, one of her guns exploded, killing, among others, Secretary of State Abel P. Upshur(1791–1844) and Secretary of the Navy Thomas W. Gilmer (1802–1844). Although Ericsson was not responsible for the disaster, he was blamed for it. In the fall of 1861, the federal government commissioned him to construct an armored warship "for the destruction of the Rebel fleet." Ericsson turned to the project with great energy and launched the *Monitor* in the incredible time of 100 working days. On March 9, 1862, the *Monitor* fought the Southern ironclad, the *Merrimack,* to a draw (*see* Battle of the *Monitor* **and** *Merrimack*). The *Monitor* made Ericsson a national hero, and he designed and built several other armored ships during the

John Ericsson

war. Later, he designed a fleet of gunboats for Spain and developed a warship that shot torpedoes under water. During his last years, Ericsson worked with electric engines and sought ways to harness the energy of the sun.

EWELL, Richard Stoddert (1817–1872). As commander of Robert E. Lee's Second Corps, this one-legged Confederate officer led the Southern advance through the Shenandoah Valley to Gettysburg in 1863 strapped to his horse. After graduating from West Point in 1840, Ewell served on the frontier and in the war with Mexico. In May, 1861, he resigned his commission in the federal army and was appointed a colonel in the Confederate Army. A month later, he was promoted to brigadier general. That July, he fought in the First Battle of Bull Run and three months later was promoted to major general. In the summer of 1862, Ewell lost a leg in the Second Battle of Bull Run. Promoted to lieutenant general, he returned to active duty with a wooden leg in May, 1863. When the Confederate Army was divided into three corps after the Battle of Chancellorsville in May, 1863, Ewell took command of the Second Corps, which he led at the Battle of Gettysburg on July 1–3, 1863. The next year, he opposed Union General **Ulysses S. Grant** (*see*) in the first engagement of the Battle of the Wilderness and two weeks later was in the Battle of Spotsylvania Court House on May 19, 1864. Ewell's horse was shot from under him at Spotsylvania, and the injuries he suffered left him unfit for further field service. He was subsequently put in command of the defenses of Richmond. Southern forces abandoned the city in the first days of April, 1865, starting fires at warehouses and other strategic points that soon enveloped the entire business district. Ewell, who was blamed for the destruction, was captured at Sayler's Creek on April 6, 1865, and imprisoned for four months. Following his release, Ewell retired to live on his farm near Spring Hill, Tennessee.

F

FARRAGUT, David Glasgow (1801–1870). Farragut was the most outstanding Union naval commander in the Civil War and America's first admiral. Born in Tennessee, he followed his father and brother into the navy at the age of nine. He saw his first action during the War of 1812, and although only 12 years old, he was put in charge of returning to port a British ship captured in the Pacific Ocean. Afterward, he rose slowly to the rank of commander, seeing duty in the Mediterranean Sea and the West Indies. During the Mexican War, Farragut asked to be relieved of duty because he had been given unimportant blockading assignments.

David G. Farragut

He spent the years between 1850 and the outbreak of the Civil War mostly in performing various shore duties. When Virginia seceded from the Union in 1861, Farragut left his home in Norfolk and moved to New York State. His Southern descent prevented him from getting an appointment in the navy until the next year, when he was given a squadron and ordered to capture New Orleans. The city was heavily defended by two forts and a Confederate flotilla. When Farragut's mortar vessels failed to bombard the forts into surrender, he ordered his 17 ships to run by them. Despite a crippling barrage, all but three ships got past. His squadron then destroyed 11 ships of the Confederate flotilla beyond the forts and captured New Orleans on April 25. This brilliant operation made Farragut a national hero overnight. He subsequently took part in the siege of Vicksburg in 1863 and the next year set out to capture Mobile, Alabama, an important port for Confederate blockade runners. Mobile was guarded by two powerful forts on sandspits at the

entrance to the harbor. The channel into the harbor was sealed off with 180 floating mines, then called torpedoes. Farragut led his fleet of 18 ships into the bay on the morning of August 5. When the ironclad *Tecumseh* struck a mine and sank, the other ships fell into confusion. Farragut, standing in the rigging of his flagship, shouted, "Damn the torpedoes! Full speed ahead!" The line of Union ships straightened out and steamed into the bay over the mines, which failed to explode. The ships sailed past the forts and dispersed the Confederate fleet there. Both forts later surrendered. Farragut saw no more fighting after that action. He was commissioned vice admiral in 1864 and admiral two years later—ranks that were especially created for him. In 1867, he made a goodwill tour as commander of the European Squadron.

FIFTEENTH AMENDMENT. Passed to fortify the **Fourteenth Amendment** (*see*) and to enforce the right of blacks to vote in the South, the Fifteenth Amendment begins, "The right of citizens of the United States to vote shall not be denied or abridged by the United States or by any State on account of race, color, or previous condition of servitude." A second section declares that "The Congress shall have power to enforce this article by appropriate legislation." The amendment, proposed on February 27, 1869, and officially ratified on March 30, 1870, was provoked by the illegal methods by which blacks were prevented from voting in the Southern states, particularly Louisiana and Georgia. Former slaves were frequently disqualified by election officials on one pretext or another, usually having to do with voter reg-

ANNE S. K. BROWN MILITARY COLLECTION

istration. Or they were frightened from the polls by hooded members of the **Ku Klux Klan** (*see*), who whipped, occasionally murdered, and generally terrorized any blacks showing the inclination to vote. Despite the amendment, Southern states were able to ignore its provisions after the Reconstruction period because of the lack of federal enforcement. The Voting Rights Act of 1965 was passed to implement this amendment.

FISH, Hamilton (1808–1893). Unlike many of the men in the cabinet of President **Ulysses S. Grant** (*see*), Fish was honest, able, and statesmanlike. As Secretary of State (1869–1877), he negotiated with Britain the Treaty of Washington, which led to the settlement of boundary and fishing-rights disputes with Canada, and also arranged for the arbitration of American claims arising out of the Civil War. This treaty was signed in May, 1871, after two years of skillful negotiations. Two years later, Fish was successful in averting war with Spain when the *Virginius,* a ship flying the American flag but manned by Cuban revolutionaries, was seized by Spanish authorities and 54 Americans among the crew and passengers were executed. Fish showed that the ship had been illegally registered as an American vessel and won $80,000 in damages for the executed men's heirs. Fish's years as Secretary of State capped a career spent almost entirely in politics. He left a law practice in New York City to serve a term in the House of Representatives in 1843 and was elected governor of New York five years later. Fish, a Whig and a moderate on the slavery issue, returned to Washington as a Senator in 1851. After spend-

ing two years in Europe at the expiration of his Senate term in 1857, Fish became a Republican and campaigned for **Abraham Lincoln** (*see*) in the 1860 election. During the Civil War, he worked on New York State's defense committee and as a federal commissioner for the relief of war prisoners. Although he at first declined Grant's offer of the post of Secretary of State in 1869 and thereafter repeatedly offered to resign the post, Fish remained in office until 1877, serving the longest of any of Grant's cabinet members. Both before and after his cabinet service, he was chairman of the board of trustees of Columbia College in New York City.

FOOTE, Andrew Hull (1806–1863). Foote, who left West Point in 1822 to join the navy, helped to win control of the Mississippi River for the Union early in the Civil War. A native of Connecticut, Foote was known as a temperance reformer. While serving as executive officer on the U. S. S. *Cumberland* in the early 1840s, he formed a ship's temperance society and banned the grog (rum-drink) ration that seamen were customarily given each day. His zeal finally led to the navy's abandoning its alcohol rations in 1862. Foote fought slave traders off the coast of Africa from 1849 to 1851. In 1856, while commanding an American warship off Canton, China, he stormed and destroyed four barrier forts below the city after the forts had fired on his ship. In the Civil War, Foote commanded naval operations on the upper Mississippi River, and his gunboats helped the Union Army take Fort Henry and Fort Donelson in Tennessee in 1862. Foote was wounded in the attack on

Fort Donelson and saw no more combat after that. He was named to command the Union squadron blockading Charleston, South Carolina, in 1863 but died before he could reach his new post.

FORREST, Nathan Bedford (1821–1877). One of the greatest Confederate cavalry officers of the Civil War, Tennessee-born Nathan Forrest was famous for his brilliant raids on Union lines, supplies, communications, and garrisons. Union General **William T. Sherman** (*see*) described him as "the most remarkable man the Civil War produced on either side." Forrest, who began his career as a humble farm laborer, was a wealthy cotton planter by the outbreak of the Civil War. In June, 1861, he enlisted as a private in the Confederate Army and was made a colonel the following October, after he had organized and equipped a cavalry battalion at his own expense. He subsequently fought at Fort Donelson, Shiloh, and Murfreesboro. In July, 1862, Forrest was made a brigadier general and began his famed cavalry raids. He took part in the Chattanooga campaign and was appointed a major general in December, 1863. On April 12, 1864, Forrest captured Fort Pillow, Tennessee, and some historians believe that he was responsible for ordering the massacre of many black Union soldiers after that garrison had surrendered. During Sherman's Atlanta campaign (May–September, 1864), Forrest continued his raids, winning a notable victory at Brices Cross Roads, Mississippi, and fighting an inconclusive battle at Tupelo, Mississippi. During the Nashville campaign in November and December, 1864, Forrest was chief Confederate cavalry commander, and in

February, 1865, he was made a lieutenant general. He was finally defeated at Selma, Alabama, in early April and surrendered the following month. Forrest subsequently became an active member of the **Ku Klux Klan** (*see*), serving as its Grand Wizard from 1867 to 1869, and was also involved in building railroads.

FOURTEENTH AMENDMENT.

This amendment, a product of the postwar Reconstruction Era, made blacks citizens of the United States and transferred the protection of individual liberties from the states to the federal government. It excluded "active" Confederates from public life and also canceled all debts incurred by the Confederate government or individual states of the Confederacy. Formulated by the Joint Congressional Committee on Reconstruction, the amendment was passed by the House of Representatives in May, 1866, by the Senate the following month, and ratified by the states on July 28, 1868. The first of five sections of the amendment repudiated the Supreme Court's Dred Scott decision of 1857 by making blacks "citizens of the United States and of the State wherein they reside." It further prohibited the states from abridging the rights of any citizens and declared that "no state shall deprive any person of life, liberty, or property, without due process of law; nor deny to any person within its jurisdiction the equal protection of the laws." This section incorporated the earlier **Civil Rights Act of 1866** (*see*), whose constitutionality was in doubt. The second section of the amendment safeguarded the suffrage of all males by penalizing any state that withheld their right to vote by proportionately reduc-

ing that state's representation in Congress. This section was designed to force the states to allow blacks to vote in state and federal elections. Section three of the amendment disqualified from state or federal office anyone who had, as a state or federal official, taken an oath to support the Constitution and thereafter "engaged in insurrection or rebellion." This section was to exclude "unreconstructed rebels" from state or federal office, though it also provided that a two-thirds vote of Congress could remove the disability. The fourth section of this amendment validated the Union war debts and repudiated the Confederacy's debts. The fifth and last section empowered Congress to enforce the amendment by appropriate legislation. Although originally designed to protect blacks, the Fourteenth Amendment has since been used to protect corporations, legally regarded as "persons," from being deprived of property by state action without due process of law.

FRITCHIE, Barbara (1776–1865). Legend has it that this 86-year-old woman defiantly waved the Union flag at General **Stonewall Jackson** (*see*) and his Confederate troops as they passed through Frederick, Maryland, on September 6, 1862. Two years later, the poet John Greenleaf Whittier (1807–1892) dedicated a patriotic ballad to Mrs. Fritchie, thereby immortalizing her name. As Whittier described the event, when the Confederates fired upon the flag, Mrs. Fritchie caught it before it fell: " 'Shoot, if you must, this old gray head,/ But spare your country's flag,' she said." Impressed by this act of patriotism, the general, according to Whittier, ordered his soldiers to leave the flag alone.

Later evidence indicated that a Mrs. Mary A. Quantrill, a relative of the Southern raider **William Quantrill** (*see*), had been the one who flaunted the Union standard at the Confederates. It was only after Jackson's soldiers had left Frederick and the Union Army had entered a few days later that Mrs. Fritchie was presented with a flag to wave. A Mrs. E. D. E. N. Southworth, a local novelist, is credited with sending the erroneous information to Whittier.

G

GETTYSBURG ADDRESS. The

Gettysburg Address was delivered by President **Abraham Lincoln** (*see*) on November 19, 1863, at the dedication ceremony of a national cemetery on the battlefield of Gettysburg, Pennsylvania, the site of the Civil War's greatest combat (July 1–3, 1863). The main speaker at the ceremony was the statesman and orator Edward Everett (1794–1865). His two-hour oration has been forgotten, while Lincoln's five-minute speech has become world famous. Lincoln, who had written most of his address in Washington, D.C., made some revisions at Gettysburg. He began with a reference to American tradition: "Four score and seven years ago our fathers brought forth, on this continent, a new nation, conceived in Liberty, and dedicated to the proposition that all men are created equal." He ended with the exhortation "that this nation, under God, shall have a new birth of freedom—and that government of the people, by the people, for the people, shall not perish from the earth." Many people present criticized and denounced the President's address for partisan reasons. However, others appreciated its literary merits and recognized that it was the perfect expression of the nation's democratic ideal.

GRANT, Ulysses Simpson (1822–1885). As general-in-chief of the Union Army, Grant engineered the military defeat of the Confederacy in the Civil War and became a national hero. However, later, as the 18th President (1869–1877) of the United States, the politically inexperienced Grant saw his administration disgraced by corruption and scandal. Born Hiram Ulysses in Point Pleasant, Ohio, Grant was mistakenly registered as Ulysses Simpson when he was appointed to West Point in 1839. He accepted the change to avoid teasing because of his real initials (H. U. G.). The initials of his adopted name later gave rise to his being called Uncle Sam and Unconditional Surrender. After graduation in 1843, Grant served ably in the Mexican War. He was then stationed in California and Oregon for several years, but heavy drinking forced him to resign from the army in 1854. He engaged in unprofitable farming and real-estate ventures in St. Louis (1854–1860) before becoming a clerk in a family store in Galena, Illinois. With the outbreak of the Civil War, Grant's lackluster career changed abruptly. Commissioned an officer in the Illinois volunteers, he drove the Confederates from the strategic Forts Henry and Donelson in Tennessee in early 1862, winning the rank of major general. He was first called Unconditional Surrender Grant when he rejected the Confederate defenders' proposal for an armistice. Grant's brilliant victory in the Vicksburg campaign (1862–1863), which

gave the Union control of the Mississippi River, persuaded President **Abraham Lincoln** (*see*) to name him commander of the entire Western theater of operations. After defeating the Confederates at Chattanooga, Tennessee, in November, 1863, Grant was appointed general-in-chief of all Union forces, becoming the first person to hold that rank since

Grant confers with two aides at his headquarters at Cold Harbor, Virginia, in 1864.

COLLECTION OF LLOYD OSTENDORF

George Washington (1732–1799). Grant replaced incompetent generals with such capable men as **William T. Sherman, Philip Sheridan,** and **George H. Thomas** (*see all*). Despite heavy Union casualties—for which he was called the Butcher—he wore down the army of **Robert E. Lee** (*see*) by applying constant pressure in 1864–1865 in the Wilderness campaign and the siege of Petersburg, Virginia. Lee, finally trapped near Appomattox, Virginia, surrendered on April 9, 1865. Grant was elected

President on the Republican ticket in 1868 and reelected four years later, although he was unsuited for the Presidency. He appointed many unfit men to his cabinet. Personally honest, he was repeatedly deceived by false friends, who used his prestige and power to advance their own selfish and illegal schemes. Among those implicated in corrupt dealings during Grant's administration were Vice-President **Schuyler Colfax** (*see*), the Attorney General, the Secretaries of War, the Treasury, and the Interior, and Grant's private secretary, **Orville E. Babcock** (*see*). Grant's second term of office saw the financial Panic of 1873 and the ensuing depression. In foreign affairs, however, much was accomplished by his able Secretary of State, **Hamilton Fish** (*see*). After leaving office in 1877, Grant toured Europe for two years before settling in New York City.

Bankrupt because of unwise investments, and suffering from cancer of the throat, Grant wrote his famous *Personal Memoirs* to obtain money to provide for his family. The manuscript, which eventually netted his heirs almost $500,000, was finished a few days before his death on July 23, 1885.

GRIERSON, Benjamin Henry (1826–1911). As a Union colonel, Grierson led a daring raid behind enemy lines in 1863, riding 600 miles in 16 days and destroying Confederate property and railroad tracks. Grierson, who had enlisted in the Civil War as a private, was a former music teacher and merchant. He rose rapidly to command in the Illinois cavalry. During the campaign of General **Ulysses S. Grant** (*see*) to capture Vicksburg, Mississippi, in 1863, Grierson commanded about 1,700 horse soldiers. He left La Grange, Tennessee, on April 17, 1863, and rode through Mississippi—at one point fighting off three companies of rebel cavalry—before reaching his goal, Baton Rouge, Louisiana, on May 2. His raid, which drew Southern forces away from Vicksburg, was called by Grant "one of the most brilliant cavalry exploits of the war, and will be handed down in history as an example to be imitated." President **Abraham Lincoln** (*see*) promoted Grierson to major general for "his great raid through the heart of the so-called Confederacy." After the war, he led campaigns against Indians in the West and commanded units in Texas, Arizona, and New Mexico. He retired in 1890.

H

HALLECK, Henry (1815–1872). Halleck, who graduated third in his West Point class of 1839 and won the nickname Old Brains for his studiousness, was more successful as an administrator than as a field commander. A native of New York, he had retired from the army in 1854 and become a lawyer before the Civil War broke out. After **Abraham Lincoln** (*see*) appointed him a major general in 1861, he commanded armies in Missouri, Ohio, Kansas, Kentucky, and Tennessee for several months. In 1862, Halleck was brought to Washington, D.C., as military adviser to President Lincoln. Besides the shortcomings he showed in his handling of battle strategy, he also antagonized politicians and his fellow officers. In 1864, General **Ulysses S. Grant** (*see*) took over as commander in chief of the Union's armies, and Halleck was demoted to the less important office of chief of staff. After the war, he commanded divisions in California and Kentucky. The strain and pressures of his wartime years in the capital helped to bring on his death in 1872.

HAMLIN, Hannibal (1809–1891). This Maine Republican was Vice-President (1861–1865) in the first administration of **Abraham Lincoln** (*see*). A lawyer, Hamlin was first elected to the House to represent Maine in 1843, and after two terms became a Senator in 1848. He spoke out strongly against slavery and joined the new Republican Party in 1856. He was elected governor of Maine that year but resigned after a month in office to reenter the Senate. There he became one of the leaders of the anti-slavery forces and in 1860 was chosen as Lincoln's running mate. As Vice-President, Hamlin complained about "the slow and unsatisfactory movements of the gov-ernment" toward freeing slaves. Partly because of his lack of moderation, he was not picked to run again with Lincoln in 1864. He was reelected to the Senate in 1868, serving until he was appointed minister to Spain in 1881. After a year abroad, Hamlin returned to Maine, where he was influential in Republican Party politics.

HAMPTON, Wade (1818–1902). A wealthy South Carolina planter who opposed secession, Hampton nevertheless used part of his fortune to equip the Hampton Legion—a unit made up of infantry, cavalry, and artillery troops that fought in the Confederate Army. He was wounded several times in battle—first at the First Battle of Bull Run, Virginia, in July, 1861, and then at the Battle of Seven Pines, Virginia, in June, 1862. Promoted to major general, Hampton led cavalry troops into battle at Antietam, Maryland, in September, 1862, and at Gettysburg, Pennsylvania, in July, 1863, where he was wounded for a third time. After the death of General **Jeb Stuart** (*see*) in 1864, Hampton, who had been Stuart's second in command, took over the cavalry corps. He fought the rest of the war on the defensive, partly because of a shortage of horses. After the war, Hampton returned to South Carolina to find that he had lost much of his fortune. He was twice elected governor (1876–1879) of his state and then served in the United States Senate (1879–1891). Throughout the postwar years, Hampton was the major figure in South Carolina politics. His leadership in restoring home rule in his state made him a hero to his people.

HANCOCK, Winfield Scott (1824–1886). One of the great

Union generals during the Civil War, Hancock ran for the Presidency in 1880 and was narrowly beaten by James A. Garfield (1831–1881). Hancock graduated from West Point in 1844. He fought in the Mexican War and then against the Seminole Indians in Florida and in the Kansas border wars. At the outbreak of the Civil War, Hancock was appointed a brigadier general in charge of training the Army of the Potomac. He served under General **George McClellan** (*see*) at Antietam in 1862, and the following year, the courage and discipline of his troops saved the Union forces from total disaster at the Battle of Chancellorsville. Hancock himself chose the ground on which the Battle of Gettysburg was fought on July 1–3, 1863. He defeated Confederate efforts to turn the federal flank on the second day of the battle and stopped the Confederate attack on the Union center on the third, suffering a severe wound. Hancock remained in the army after the war. He was nominated by the Democratic Party to run against Garfield, a Republican, in 1880 but received only 155 electoral votes to Garfield's 214. Afterward, Hancock returned to his military duties, serving until his death.

HARDEE, William Joseph (1815–1873). Hardee commanded the Southern forces that tried to stop Union General **William T. Sherman** (*see*) in his march across Georgia and South Carolina in 1864–1865. A West Point graduate (1838), Hardee early in his career wrote a book called *Rifle and Light Infantry Tactics,* later popularly known as *Hardee's Tactics.* It became a textbook for the United States Army. He was on leave from his post as commandant of cadets at West Point when his home state of Georgia left the Union in January, 1861. Hardee became a major general and later a lieutenant general in the Confederate Army and fought at Shiloh, Tennessee, Perryville, Kentucky, and in other battles in the West in 1862 and 1863. Hardee was regarded highly as a battle leader by both Southern and Northern commanders. Sherman called him a "competent soldier." After the war, Hardee retired to a farm in Alabama.

HAYES, Rutherford Birchard (1822–1893). The 19th President of the United States, Hayes received fewer popular votes than his opponent, **Samuel J. Tilden** (*see*), in the 1876 election, but was chosen President by one electoral vote. Once in office, he withdrew federal troops from the South and ended the corrupt era of Reconstruction (*see* **Reconstruction Acts**). The son of an Ohio shopkeeper, Hayes attended Harvard Law School, graduating in 1845. That same year, in order to live away from his overly affectionate and unstable sister, he moved to the small town of Lower Sandusky (now Fremont) to practice law. In 1849, he settled in Cincinnati, where he became known for his participation in several sensational criminal cases. Seven years later, Hayes helped to found the Ohio Republican Party, and in 1858 he became city solicitor. Hayes enlisted in the Union Army at the outbreak of the Civil War. He was wounded five times and rose to the rank of major general. Hayes was elected to the House of Representatives in 1864 and took his seat in it after the war had ended. Depressed by the widespread political corruption of the time, he was glad to leave Wash-

Hayes boasted of his devotion to duty and was elected to Congress in 1864.

ington when he was nominated to be governor of Ohio in 1867. During his three terms (1868–1872, 1876–1877) in office, he worked for reforms in the state administration. In 1876, Hayes was nominated for President by the Republican Party. In his letter of acceptance he pledged himself toward "a civil policy which will wipe out forever the distinction between North and South in our common country." After a confusing and bitterly fought election, Hayes received about 250,000 votes less than his opponent, Tilden. However, the electoral votes of several states were disputed and a special commission was set up to settle the question. Supreme Court Justice **Joseph P. Bradley** (*see*) cast the deciding vote, and all the disputed votes were awarded to Hayes. In all, he received 185 electoral votes, only one more than Tilden. Hayes became President of a nation still torn by the sectional differences that had helped to kindle the Civil War. He immediately embarked on a program of Southern pacification. Within weeks, he had removed all federal troops from the Southern states and appointed former Confederates to government posts. He helped to allocate funds to public projects in the South and restored that section of the country to relative peace and prosperity for the first time since the Civil War. He was unsuccessful, however, in trying to end the political spoils system and get civil-service reforms enacted. Hayes did not seek reelection. He retired from politics in 1881 to devote the remainder of his life to education and prison reforms. He died on January 17, 1893.

HILL, Ambrose Powell (1825–1865). Virginia-born A. P. Hill was credited with rescuing the troops of **Robert E. Lee** (*see*) at Antietam in 1862 by a swift flanking attack upon federal forces. In 1847, the year of his graduation from West Point, he saw action in the Mexican War and later served in the Seminole campaigns of 1849–1850 and 1853–1855. When Virginia seceded from the Union in 1861, Hill resigned from the federal army and entered the Confederate service as a colonel of the 13th Virginia Infantry. He was subsequently promoted to lieutenant general. After the Battles of Mechanicsville and Frazier's Farm in June, 1862, his troops were dubbed Hill's Light Division because of the speed with which he was able to get his men into action. For a year thereafter, he commanded the Light Division as part of the Army of Northern Virginia. In addition to aiding Lee at Antietam in September, 1862, Hill and his Light Division were of great help to **Stonewall Jack-**

son (*see*) at Chancellorsville in April–May, 1863. Later that year, Hill took command of one of the three corps into which Lee had divided his army for its invasion north through the Shenandoah Valley into Pennsylvania. Hill was killed on April 2, 1865, the same day he returned from a sick leave to Petersburg, Virginia, then under federal assault. Both Lee and Jackson had held him in high esteem. Lee's last, delirious words before his own death five years later were, "Tell A. P. Hill he must come up."

HILL, Daniel Harvey (1821–1889). D. H. Hill divided his career between education and military service. A West Point graduate (1842), he served in the Mexican War but left the army in 1849 to teach mathematics at Washington College (now Washington and Lee University) in Virginia. After the Civil War began, Hill became a Confederate general and fought under General **Robert E. Lee** (*see*) at the Seven Days' Battles in Virginia in the summer of 1862. After the failure of the Confederate Chattanooga campaign in 1863, Hill and other Southern generals recommended that General **Braxton Bragg** (*see*) be relieved of command because of incompetence. However, the Confederate President, **Jefferson Davis** (*see*), sided with Bragg and removed Hill instead. Hill did not see active duty again until the last days of the war. After it was over, Hill founded a Southern magazine, *The Land We Love,* in 1866 and later became president (1877–1884) of the University of Arkansas and then president (1885–1889) of the Middle Georgia Military and Agricultural College (now Georgia Military College). As an educator, Hill en-

couraged training in industry and agriculture as ways to rebuild the South.

HOOD, John Bell (1831–1879). Commander of the "Texas Brigade," Hood contributed importantly to Confederate victories in the early stages of the Civil War. His much-praised fighting ability, however, was not matched by a grasp of military strategy, and he was soundly defeated by General **William T. Sherman** (*see*) at Atlanta, Georgia, in September, 1864. Hood, a native of Kentucky, graduated from West Point in 1853. He saw duty in California and Texas before resigning in 1861 to accept a lieutenant's commission in the Confederate Army. Hood served ably in the Peninsular campaign and at the Second Battle of Bull Run and quickly rose to brigadier general. A severe arm wound suffered at the Battle of Gettysburg in July, 1863, and the loss of a leg at the Battle of Chickamauga in Tennessee that September failed to halt "the Gallant Hood," who rode into battle thereafter strapped to his saddle. In July, 1864, when the defense of Atlanta was going badly, Confederate President **Jefferson Davis** (*see*) named Hood to replace General **Joseph E. Johnston** (*see*) as commander of the Army of Tennessee. However, Hood lost the fight for Atlanta that September and was again crushed three months later in the battle for Nashville, Tennessee. He resigned his command in January, 1865, and surrendered in Mississippi that May. After the war, Hood entered business in New Orleans. He died during a yellow-fever outbreak.

HOOKER, Joseph (1814–1879). Hooker commanded the Union

Army of the Potomac in early 1863, but he was relieved after the Confederate victory at Chancellorsville, Virginia. A West Point graduate (1837), Hooker served in the Mexican War before resigning from the army in 1853 to farm in California. He rejoined the federal army at the outbreak of the Civil War. In June, 1862, his division bore the brunt of the fighting at Williamsburg, Virginia, during the Peninsular campaign. Hooker, at the head of his troops during the entire battle, displayed such bravery that he earned the nickname Fighting Joe. When **Ambrose Burnside** (*see*), the commander of the Army of the Potomac, lost the Battle of Fredericksburg the following December, Hooker was strongly critical of Burnside's leadership. Early in 1863, **Abraham Lincoln** (*see*) relieved Burnside and gave Hooker the post. At the same time, however, Lincoln admonished Hooker, saying, "I believe you to be a brave and skillful soldier . . . [but] I much fear that the spirit which you have aided to infuse into the army, of criticizing their commander . . . will now turn upon you." Boldly proclaiming, "May God have mercy on General Lee, for I will have none," Hooker led his troops to bloody defeat by a force half the size of his own at Chancellorsville in May. Although he skillfully tracked **Robert E. Lee** (*see*) to Gettysburg, Hooker resigned his command on the eve of the battle there after a dispute with **Henry Halleck** (*see*) over reinforcements and was replaced by **George Gordon Meade** (*see*). Hooker subsequently fought bravely in the West with smaller commands, but he was passed up for promotion and was relieved from field service at his own request in September, 1864. He retired from the army in 1868, after suffering a paralytic stroke.

HOWE, Julia Ward (1819–1910). Mrs. Howe's stirring *Battle Hymn of the Republic* was one of the favorite marching songs of the Union Army and today is one of the nation's most patriotic songs. A vivacious New York socialite and heiress, Julia Ward married Dr. Samuel Gridley Howe (1801–1876), a social reformer and philanthropist, in 1843. Their Boston home, called Green Peace, soon became a center of abolitionist activity prior to the Civil War. During this period, the Howes edited *The Commonwealth*, an antislavery journal, and Mrs. Howe published her first volume of poetry, *Passion Flowers* (1854). When the war started, Dr. Howe was appointed a member of the United States Sanitary Commission, a forerunner of the American Red Cross, in Washington, D.C. At a picnic outside that city on November 18, 1861, Mrs. Howe witnessed an unexpected attack on Union troops by Southern skirmishers. The experience deeply moved her. The next day, as she later explained, "[I] awoke in the gray of the morning twilight, and as I lay waiting for the dawn, the long lines of the poem began to twine themselves" in her mind. When her five-stanza poem was published in the February, 1862, issue of *The Atlantic Monthly*, Mrs. Howe received only $4 but gained national fame. Set to the tune of *John Brown's Body*, a song composed the previous decade by William Steffe, the *Battle Hymn* was an immediate success. It soon became a favorite song among the Union troops, and on one occasion, President Lincoln stood, tears streaming down his face, while people

BROWN BROTHERS

Although 91, Mrs. Julia Ward Howe still appeared at rallies for women's rights.

gathered at a meeting in the capital sang, "*Mine eyes have seen the glory of the coming of the Lord:/ He is trampling out the vintage where the grapes of wrath are stored;/He hath loosed the fateful lightning of His terrible swift sword:/His truth is marching on.*" After the war, Mrs. Howe campaigned for various causes, including prison reform, women's suffrage, and international peace. After founding the New England Woman's Club in 1868, she helped establish the American Woman's Suffrage Association the following year and the American Branch of the Woman's International Peace Association in 1871. Her last years were spent writing essays and lecturing for these organizations.

J

JACKSON, Thomas Jonathan ("Stonewall") (1824–1863). Jackson ranks as one of the most capable soldiers in American military history. Only **Robert E. Lee** (*see*) excelled him as a master of tactics in the Confederate Army or is more revered today as a war hero in the South. Born in Virginia, Jackson graduated from West Point in 1846, after a long struggle to overcome his poor educational background. He served in the Mexican War and then left the army in 1852 to teach at the Virginia Military Institute in Lexington. Commissioned a Confederate brigadier general shortly after the Civil War began, Jackson won his nickname at the First Battle of Bull Run on July 21, 1861. Jackson's men arrived on the battle scene just after the troops of General Barnard E. Bee (1824–1861) had been driven back by federal forces. "Look at Jackson's brigade; it stands like a stone wall!" Bee shouted. "Rally behind the Virginians." Jackson not only held the line, but also counterattacked. Jackson's campaign in the Shenandoah Valley (March–June, 1862) is regarded as a military classic. With lightninglike attacks and skillful maneuvers, his badly outnumbered army helped to divert the Union advance on Richmond, the Confederate capital. Jackson—as legendary for his religious piety and eccentric manner of dress as for his combat ability—continued his brilliant operations in Virginia during 1862 at the Second Battle of Bull Run and in the bloody engagements at Fredericksburg and Antietam. On May 2, 1863, after driving back the Union Army at Chancellorsville, Jackson was accidentally shot by one of his own men while checking his picket lines at dusk. His death, eight days later, deprived Lee of his best general. "I know not how

to replace him," Lee exclaimed.

JOHNSON, Andrew (1808–1875). The nation's 17th President, Johnson was the only Chief Executive ever impeached by Congress. Assuming the Presidency in the closing days of the Civil War, he tried to heal the nation's wounds by adopting a conciliatory policy toward the defeated South. In doing so, he enraged the Radical Republicans, who tried to remove him from office. Johnson was born in Raleigh, North Carolina. Self-educated, he became a tailor, and in 1826 he set up shop in Greeneville, Tennessee, where he soon entered politics. Identifying himself with the Jacksonian Democrats, Johnson—whose own father had been a laborer—championed the interests of the workingman and small farmer and opposed those born to wealth and privilege. He served (1843–1853) in the House of Representatives, was governor (1853–1857) of Tennessee, and became a Senator in 1857. Although Johnson supported legislation extending slavery in United States territory and had allied himself with the Southern faction of the Democratic Party in 1860, he was the only Southern Democrat to remain in the Senate after his own state of Tennessee seceded from the Union in 1861. As a result, he was labeled a traitor in the South and became a hero of Northern liberals. **Abraham Lincoln** (*see*) appointed him military governor of Tennessee in 1862, and Johnson was so successful in wresting the state from the Confederates that Lincoln chose him as his running mate two years later. When Lincoln was assassinated on April 14, 1865, less than five weeks after his second inauguration, Johnson suddenly found himself President

Critics ridiculed Johnson's use of the Constitution in his impeachment trial.

during one of the most difficult periods in the nation's history. At first he followed Lincoln's plan for reconstruction by restoring local governments in the secessionist states and offering amnesty to former Confederates. However, his moderate policy toward the South and his conservative view that civil rights for blacks should be established by individual state laws antagonized the Radical Republicans, who demanded harsh punishment for the South. The Radicals, who controlled Congress, repeatedly overrode the President's vetoes on the **Civil Rights Act of 1866,** the **Reconstruction Acts,** and the **Tenure of Office Act** (*see all*). In open defiance of the Tenure of Office Act, Johnson dismissed his Secretary of War, **Edwin Stanton** (*see*), without Congressional consent in 1867. The House of Representatives subsequently instituted impeachment proceedings against Johnson for violating his oath of office and being guilty of "high crimes and misdemeanors." At the three-month trial, beginning in March, 1868, the dramatic arguments of the Radical Republicans were torn to shreds by Johnson's attorneys. The final Senate vote of 35 to 19 was just one vote short of the necessary two-thirds majority needed for conviction. After completing his term as President, Johnson twice campaigned unsuccessfully for the Senate but was finally elected a Senator from Tennessee in 1874. He died in Carter Station, Tennessee, on July 31, 1875, just a few months after taking his seat.

JOHNSTON, Albert Sidney (1803–1862). A Southern general who was considered one of the greatest military leaders of his time, Johnston was killed on the first day of the Battle of Shiloh in Tennessee in April, 1862. A Kentuckian, Johnston graduated from West Point in 1826, served in the Black Hawk War in 1832, and then resigned from the army to farm in Texas. In 1835, he enlisted in the Texas revolutionary army and rose to become its commander and, later, the secretary of war in the Republic of Texas. Johnston fought in the Mexican War and then rejoined the United States Army and served as commander of forces in Texas and Utah. When the Civil War broke out, Johnston was commanding the Department of the Pacific in San Francisco. The federal government offered him a high command in the Union Army, but Johnston, upset by false reports that he planned to deliver California over to the Confederacy, refused the offer. In August, 1861, he became a Confederate general and took command of forces in the West. Johnston had great difficulty in finding enough men

for his army, and his outnumbered troops were defeated at the Battle of Mill Springs in Kentucky and then lost Forts Henry and Donelson in Tennessee to General **Ulysses S. Grant** (*see*). Nevertheless, **Jefferson Davis** (*see*), the President of the Confederacy, refused to replace him, declaring, "If Sidney Johnston is not a general, I have none." At Shiloh on April 6, 1862, Johnston was wounded while leading his army and bled to death. He was buried in New Orleans, but after the war, his remains were carried to Texas for reburial in Austin. General **Philip Sheridan** (*see*) would not allow a military funeral procession to be held. However, Johnston's friends showed their respects by silently following the coffin through the streets of several Texas cities as it was taken to Austin.

JOHNSTON, Joseph Eggleston (1807–1891). A Confederate general who fought and was defeated by General **William T. Sherman** (*see*) in Georgia, Johnston died 26 years after the war when he caught pneumonia while standing hatless at Sherman's funeral. An expert in defensive warfare, Johnston fought the Seminoles in Florida after graduating from West Point in 1829 and also served with distinction in the Mexican War. A native of Virginia, he resigned as quartermaster general of the army at the outbreak of the Civil War to fight for the Confederacy. Early in the war, he eluded a Union force at Harpers Ferry, Virginia, and then aided in the Southern victory at the First Battle of Bull Run, which earned him the command of the army in northern Virginia. Johnston was wounded twice at the Battle of Seven Pines in Virginia in 1862.

After he recovered, he was given command of the rebel forces in the West. After several defeats in Tennessee and at Vicksburg, Mississippi, in 1863, Johnston took command of the Army of the Tennessee. He skillfully defended Georgia against Sherman, but Sherman, with an army twice the size of Johnston's, outmaneuvered him and finally captured Atlanta in 1864. On April 26, 1865, 17 days after the surrender of General **Robert E. Lee** (*see*) at Appomattox, Johnston surrendered his forces to Sherman. Throughout the war, Johnston carried on a feud with **Jefferson Davis** (*see*), the Confederate President, who prevented the general from carrying out several of his plans. In the postwar years, Johnston served one term in the House of Representatives (1879–1881) and later was a federal commissioner of railroads (1885–1891).

K

KU KLUX KLAN. This secret society, which began and flourished in the South during the postwar Reconstruction Era, was founded by former Confederates and dedicated to maintaining "white supremacy" by intimidating newly emancipated slaves. After the Civil War, the Radical Republicans in Congress had enacted **Reconstruction Acts** (*see*) that deprived Southern leaders of the vote and of control of their local governments. This aroused widespread fear that blacks would vote according to Republican dictates. Although many committees of Southerners were formed to rectify their grievances, the Ku Klux Klan, organized in 1866 at Pulaski, Tennessee, was the most famous.

Within a year, its membership rose rapidly, and at its convention in Nashville in 1867 a constitution for the "Invisible Empire of the South" was adopted. Former Confederate General **Nathan Forrest** (*see*) was chosen as president, or Grand Wizard. Klansmen—clad in white robes, masks, and tall conical hats to escape detection by federal troops—rode through the countryside at night terrorizing superstitious blacks, who thought the riders were Confederate ghosts. They set homes on fire and flogged and hanged their black owners. By 1869, law-abiding Southerners, revolted by these tactics, ordered the Klan to disband. However, it continued to operate and in 1871 still claimed 500,000 members. Congress, in that year, passed an act empowering the President to use force to maintain law and order in the South. Although Congress compiled 13 volumes of testimony against Klansmen and more than 7,000 members were indicted, few of the accused were convicted. The Klan's activities finally subsided when Southerners regained political power. In the 1920s, there was a brief resurgence of the Ku Klux Klan, but this time its hostilities were directed primarily against Roman Catholics, Jews, and immigrants. It still exists, outside the law, in several states, north and south.

L

LEE, Robert Edward (1807–1870). The greatest Southern hero of the Civil War and considered one of the ablest generals in American history, Lee (*see p. 666*) commanded the famed Army of Northern Virginia for three years of the war. The son of the famous revolutionary cavalry officer and governor of Virginia, Henry ("Light-Horse Harry") Lee (1756–1818), Lee was born in Westmoreland County, Virginia. He graduated second in his class from West Point in 1829 and later fought with distinction in the Mexican War. Lee was superintendent of West Point (1852–1855) and then he served frontier duty in Texas (1856–1857 and 1860–1861). In 1859, Lee commanded the federal forces that captured the abolitionist John Brown (1800–1859) at Harpers Ferry, Virginia (now in West Virginia). Although Lee was devoted to the Union and unsympathetic toward slavery, his first loyalty was to his state. He was offered command of the Union Army at the outbreak of the Civil War, but when Virginia seceded in April, 1861, he resigned from the federal army and became commander of the state's military and naval forces. Lee was military adviser to Confederate President **Jefferson Davis** (*see*) from 1861 to 1862 and was soon chosen one of the Confederacy's five full generals. Although always outnumbered and short of supplies, Lee managed to prolong the war by the skillful use of his troops. After an unsuccessful campaign in western Virginia in the summer and fall of 1861, he organized the Confederate defenses on the southeast coast. On June 1, 1862, Lee assumed command of an army that was to become the most famous fighting unit in the Confederacy. He named it the Army of Northern Virginia. Taking the offensive almost immediately, Lee saved Richmond by repulsing the Union forces under General **George B. McClellan** (*see*) in the Seven Days' Battles, June 26–July 2, 1862. He defeated the federal army at the Second Battle of Bull Run the following August 29 and 30. Lee then attempted his first invasion of the North, moving into Maryland, where he fought the bloodiest single day of the war at Antietam on September 17. Lee's army suffered losses of more than 13,000 men, while the federal army, under McClellan, lost nearly 12,500 troops. Lee was forced to retreat to Virginia. He repulsed the Union Army at Fredericksburg on December 13, 1862, and at Chancellorsville on May 2–3, 1863. Although Chancellorsville is considered Lee's most brilliant victory, **Stonewall Jackson** (*see*), his most valuable commander, was mortally wounded that same day by one of his own men. Lee was obliged to reorganize his army. His decision to renew his offensive in the North at this point, before the new officers were thoroughly familiar with their troops, is believed to have been the major mistake of his career. The resulting lack of coordination was one cause of the Confederate defeat at Gettysburg, Pennsylvania, on July 1–3, 1863. During the Wilderness campaign, May–June, 1864, Lee remained on the defensive, repulsing the federal army without being able to turn it back. Then, in the middle of June, Union General **Ulysses S. Grant** (*see*) began his nearly 10-month siege of Petersburg. By the time Lee was appointed commander in chief of all the Confederate Armies on February 6, 1865, the South was on the verge of collapse. Lee was forced to evacuate Petersburg and Richmond on April 2–3, and a week later, on April 9, he surrendered to Grant at Appomattox Court House. From October, 1865, until his death, Lee was president of Washington College in Lexington,

Virginia, which changed its name to Washington and Lee University in his honor in 1871. His estate across the Potomac River from Washington, D.C., in Arlington, Virginia, was sold for taxes during the war. His former home there, in what is now the Arlington National Cemetery, is a national museum.

LINCOLN, Abraham (*Continued from Volume 7*). Soon after Abraham Lincoln was inaugurated the 16th President of the United States on March 4, 1861, he was called upon to lead the nation through the bloody and tragic Civil War (*see pp. 655–665*). Throughout the conflict, Lincoln's main concern continued to be the preservation of the Union. The abolition of slavery remained a secondary motive, and when he spoke of emancipation, he favored repaying slave owners for their losses. He also advocated a mild policy of reconciliation toward the South after the war. Lincoln pursued these aims in the face of criticism and countless difficulties. The North suffered many humiliating military defeats during the early phase of the war, and Lincoln was forced to deal with a succession of incompetent generals before he found a capable military leader in **Ulysses S. Grant** (*see*), who became commander in chief of the Union Army in March, 1864. In addition, Lincoln's policies were opposed by several members of his own cabinet, and he was attacked by pro-Southern Peace Democrats on the one hand and by Radical Republicans, who favored harsh treatment of the South, on the other. Nevertheless, Lincoln pursued his goals singlemindedly, assuming at times almost dictatorial powers. In spite of the widespread demand for

early emancipation, he refrained from such a step because he was afraid it would alienate the slaveholding border states and because he was doubtful that slavery could be legally abolished. However, rising abolitionist sentiment in the North and in Europe prompted him to issue his **Emancipation Proclamation** (*see*) on January 1, 1863. Although this proclamation did not actually free any slaves, it had tremendous propaganda value. The few public speeches that Lincoln made as President have become world famous. His **Gettysburg Address** (*see*) of November 19, 1863, reflected his hope for reconciliation with the South. After he was reelected to a second term in November, 1864, over his Democratic opponent,

CHICAGO HISTORICAL SOCIETY

Lincoln's coffin was in the first car of the funeral train on the trip to Springfield.

George B. McClellan (*see*), Lincoln delivered an inaugural address on March 4, 1865, that remains one of his greatest orations. In it, he urged his fellow Americans to "judge not, that we be not judged." He concluded with the famous exhortation, "With malice toward none; with charity for all, let us strive on to finish the work we are in; to bind up the nation's wounds . . . to do all which may achieve and cherish

a just and lasting peace. . . ." Earlier, in the course of peace negotiations with Confederate officials at Hampton Roads, Virginia, in February, 1865, Lincoln had insisted on only two points: reunion and the abolition of slavery. Unfortunately, Lincoln did not live to put his lenient reconstruction plans into effect. On Good Friday, April 14, 1865, while attending an evening performance at Ford's Theatre in Washington, D.C., Lincoln was shot in the head by a deranged actor, **John Wilkes Booth** (*see*). He died early the following morning without regaining consciousness. At his death, Secretary of War **Edwin Stanton** (*see*) remarked, "Now he belongs to the ages." After Lincoln's body lay in state in the Rotunda of the Capitol, it was placed aboard a special seven-car funeral train on April 21. The train took nearly two weeks to reach Springfield, Illinois. Along the 1,700-mile journey, the train stopped at Philadelphia, New York, and Cleveland, where Lincoln's coffin was taken off the train and displayed publicly. Hundreds of thousands of mourners viewed it or lined the railroad tracks as the train proceeded on its solemn journey. Lincoln was laid to rest in Springfield on May 4, 1865.

LONGSTREET, James (1821–1904). A West Point graduate (1842) who consistently failed as a forceful military leader, "Old War Horse" Longstreet was perhaps the most unpopular general in the Confederate Army. Despite several successes early in the war, his mistakes cost the South victories at Fair Oaks and Seven Pines in Virginia in 1862. Later, at the Second Battle of Bull Run that same year, his infantry defeated the Union forces of General **John Pope** (*see*), but his delay in attacking deprived the South of a greater victory. Longstreet, who fought only halfheartedly when he disagreed with the plans of his superiors, commanded the Confederate right wing at Gettysburg in July, 1863. His delay again in attacking is often cited as the reason why General **Robert E. Lee** (*see*) lost that crucial battle. Longstreet later fought in the West, where he often disagreed with his fellow officers. Upon his return to Virginia, he was badly wounded in the Wilderness campaign in 1864. After the war, he criticized Lee for the defeat at Gettysburg. In addition, Longstreet, who was a friend of President **Ulysses S. Grant** (*see*), became a Republican. As a result, he was even more unpopular in the South. He spent his last years as United States minister to Turkey (1880–1881) and federal commissioner (1897–1904) of Western railroads.

M

McCLELLAN, George Brinton (1826–1885). McClellan, who be-
came commander in chief of the Union Army early in the Civil War, was hailed as the "Young Napoleon" for his brilliant administrative qualities. However, he was unable to command large forces of men effectively in battle. A native of Philadelphia, McClellan graduated from West Point in 1846 and served in the Mexican War. He resigned from the army in 1857 to become a railroad executive. He rejoined the army as a major general at the outbreak of the Civil War. His early successes, although minor, put him in the public eye, and he was made commander in chief in November, 1861. McClellan skillfully reorganized the army and made provisions for the training of recruits, but when it came to fighting, he consistently overestimated the size of the armies opposing him and was so cautious about attacking that **Abraham Lincoln** (*see*) complained that "Sending reinforcements to McClellan is like shoveling flies across a barn." Finally, early in 1862, Lincoln ordered him to advance. McClellan crept forward in the unsuccessful Peninsular campaign, an attempt to take Richmond, Virginia. Lincoln finally lost patience with McClellan when he delayed his pursuit of **Robert E. Lee** (*see*) after the Battle of Antietam in September, and replaced him with **Ambrose Burnside** (*see*). McClellan never again commanded in the field. In 1864, he ran unsuccessfully for President as a Democrat against Lincoln, losing by 400,000 votes out of 4,000,000 cast. After the war, McClellan served as governor (1878–1881) of New Jersey.

MEADE, George Gordon (1815–1872). Meade, who resigned from the army shortly after his graduation from West Point in 1835 be-
cause it offered few chances for promotion, led the Union Army to victory at the crucial Battle of Gettysburg in 1863. Meade was born in Spain, where his father, a naval agent, was stationed. He attended schools in Philadelphia and Washington, D.C., before entering West Point. After his resignation from the army in 1836, Meade worked as a civil engineer. He rejoined the army in 1842, served in the Mexican War, and fought Indians. He was also engaged in constructing lighthouses and surveying the Atlantic coast and the Great Lakes. Meade was made a brigadier general at the outbreak of the Civil War. Although wounded at the Battle of White Oak Swamp in June, 1862, Meade recovered in time to lead his men at the Second Battle of Bull Run two months later. He handled his corps boldly and skillfully at the Battle of Chancellorsville on May 24, 1863. Early in the morning of June 28, a messenger from President Lincoln awakened Meade with a letter giving him command of the exhausted Army of the Potomac—two days before the Battle of Gettysburg. Although surprised by the appointment and unfamiliar with the plans of his predecessor, **Joseph Hooker** (*see*), Meade at once began to issue orders. During the three days (July 1–3) of the battle—the greatest clash of arms on the American continent—Meade directed his troops ably and won the first great Union victory of the war. The federal success at Gettysburg is often considered the turning point of the war. Meade, however, was criticized for not pursuing the retreating Confederate Army. In the final campaigns of the war, Meade's troops were actually commanded by General **Ulysses S. Grant** (*see*), who had taken

over as the Union Army's commander in chief. After the war, Meade commanded forces on the Atlantic seaboard and briefly supervised the occupation army in the South. He died at the age of 57 of pneumonia, which was brought on by the aftereffects of the wound he had suffered in the war.

MERRIMACK. *See* ***Monitor*** **and** ***Merrimack*, Battle of the.**

MONITOR **and** *MERRIMACK,* **Battle of the.** This famous naval duel, fought on March 9, 1862, was the first battle between ironclad ships (*see p. 688*). In 1861, the Confederates raised the sunken United States steam frigate *Merrimack.* They cut her hull down to the waterline and built a sloping superstructure plated with four inches of iron and armed with six 9-inch guns and four heavy rifles. Word of this project reached the North in August, and the navy asked **John Ericsson** (*see*) to design a ship that could fight the *Merrimack.* The result was the *Monitor,* an entirely original ship with a long flat hull and a revolving iron turret that mounted two 11-inch guns. She was jeered at by Ericsson's critics as "a cheesebox on a raft." On March 8, 1862, the *Merrimack,* under the command of Franklin Buchanan (1800–1874), steamed toward Hampton Roads in Chesapeake Bay, where Union warships were blockading the James River. Impervious to the guns of the federal sailing sloop *Cumberland,* the *Merrimack* rammed and sank her. The Southern ironclad then pounded the sailing frigate *Congress* into surrender, but because it was near evening, left the big steam frigate *Minnesota* for the next day. Panic spread throughout

NEW YORK PUBLIC LIBRARY

The Monitor *and the* Merrimack *fought a four-hour duel that ended in a stalemate.*

the North. Even President **Abraham Lincoln** (*see*) feared that the Confederate ironclad might steam up the Potomac River to bombard the capital. The *Merrimack* returned the next morning to finish off the *Minnesota.* However, the *Monitor* had arrived late the night before after a grueling 48-hour sea voyage during which she was kept afloat by hand pumps and bailing. Her captain, John Worden (1818–1897), closed with the *Merrimack,* and the first Southern broadside bounced harmlessly off the *Monitor*'s turret. Neither ship was seriously damaged in the four-hour battle that followed, although at times the two vessels were actually touching. Finally, the *Merrimack* limped back to her base at Norfolk, Virginia. She was destroyed two months later when the Confederates evacuated that city. The *Monitor* sank in a gale off Cape Hatteras the following New Year's Eve, but 20 new "Monitors" were already under construction. The fiercely fought battle between the two ships had introduced a new era in naval warfare.

MORGAN, John Hunt (1825–1864). A Confederate general, Morgan fought a two-year guerrilla war against the Union Army in the West. A native of Alabama, Morgan became a suc-

cessful businessman in Kentucky after fighting in the Mexican War. In September, 1861, he joined the Confederate Army as a scout and was soon given a squadron of cavalry to command. He saw action at Shiloh in April of the following year, and three months later he led 800 men on his first raid from Tennessee into Kentucky, a border state that had remained in the Union. He lost fewer than 100 men on a 24-day operation that covered more than 1,000 miles and captured 1,200 prisoners. In the early summer of 1863, Morgan led 460 men on a raid into Kentucky, Indiana, and Ohio, destroying Union supplies and harassing the enemy forces. After a grueling 24 days of skirmishes, during which he spent an average of 21 hours a day in the saddle, he and his depleted force were finally captured in July, 1863. Morgan and his officers were put in the Ohio State Penitentiary at Columbus. Using such tools as knives from the prison dining room, Morgan and a few of his officers tunneled their way out of the prison in November, 1863. By the summer of 1864, Morgan was raiding Kentucky again. Rumors and accusations concerning atrocities committed by his men began to be leveled against him, and he was worried and unhappy when he left on his last raid late in the summer. On the morning of September 4, he was surprised by a large force of Northern cavalry in Greeneville, Tennessee. Convinced that the Union troops would try to kill him rather than take him prisoner, Morgan refused to surrender and was shot down a few minutes later.

MOSBY, John Singleton (1833–1916). During the last two years of the Civil War, Mosby conducted guerrilla raids behind the Union lines with great skill and daring. A native of Virginia, Mosby left his growing law practice to enlist in the cavalry when the Civil War broke out in 1861. He soon proved to be such a valuable scout that General **Jeb Stuart** (*see*) attached him to his staff in the spring of 1862. Mosby established his reputation by leading Stuart and 1,200 picked men on a successful three-day raid around the Union lines outside Richmond. Early in 1863, Mosby organized a squad of rangers, who supplied their own horses, food, and equipment. They moved quickly, hit hard, and scattered after each strike. His most famous exploit occurred early in the morning of March 9, 1863, when he and 30 men crept through the Union lines and captured about 30 men, including General Edwin H. Stoughton (1838–1868), and 58 horses. **Abraham Lincoln** (*see*) received news of this with the sardonic remark, "Well, I'm sorry for that. I can make new brigadier generals, but I can't make new horses." Mosby was severely wounded in December, 1864, but he recovered in time to command several operations toward the end of the war. He disbanded his rangers—who had grown to eight companies—almost two weeks after Lee surrendered at Appo-

mattox on April 9, 1865. In 1878, Mosby was appointed consul at Hong Kong, where he stayed for seven years. He returned to America to become a land agent in Colorado, and from 1904 to 1910 he was an assistant attorney for the Department of Justice. He published his memoirs in 1887.

N

NEGRO TROOPS. More than 186,000 black troops fought in the Union Army during the Civil War. Approximately half of these men came form states that had seceded. An additional 100,000 black soldiers were assigned to noncombat duties. About 29,000 blacks served in the Union Navy. The Confederacy did not

begin to enlist blacks until the war was nearly over, and none actually fought for the South. The North was at first reluctant

to accept blacks as soldiers, but military reverses in 1862 and the need for increased manpower led President **Abraham Lincoln** (*see*) to authorize widespread recruiting in 1863. Most blacks were assigned to segregated units commanded by white officers. A total of 166 all-black regiments participated in 449 separate battles. In October, 1862, the First Kansas Volunteers clashed with Confederates at Island Mounds, Missouri, in the first official action of black troops in the war. One of the most famous—and bloody—of the engagements in which black troops fought occurred at Milliken's Bend, Louisiana, in June, 1863. There, regiments of the Louisiana Volunteers of African Descent fought the longest hand-to-hand battle of the war. Another

The North recruited thousands of blacks, who served under white officers.

noted action was the siege of Fort Wagner near Charleston, South Carolina, in July, 1863. The Massachusetts Fifty-fourth Infantry attempted to storm the Confederate fort against overwhelming firepower. Again, black troops made up almost half of the 557 defenders of Fort Pillow, Tennessee, when 1,500 Confederates attacked it on April 12, 1864. The Southerners allegedly massacred most of them after the fort surrendered. Twenty-four blacks won the Medal of Honor in the Civil War, a conflict that took the lives of nearly 40,000 black soldiers.

NORTHWEST CONSPIRACY. Early in 1864, the leaders of the Confederacy conceived a desperate plan to overthrow the governments of Ohio, Illinois, Indiana, Kentucky, and Missouri. Their hope was that these states would establish a Western confederacy that would then ally itself with the South. **Jefferson Davis** (*see*), President of the Confederate States of America, dispatched three commissioners to Canada to direct the operation. They were given nearly $500,000 to arm a force to foment a rebellion. The proposed army was to consist of Confederate refugees in Canada, Confederate prisoners in Northern prison camps who would be liberated, and members of a secret pro-Southern society in the North that was named after an anti-British colonial group, the Sons of Liberty. **Clement Vallandigham** (*see*), the supreme commander of the Sons of Liberty, who was living in exile in Canada, encouraged the commissioners' plans. The date for the uprising was postponed several times but was finally set for August 29, 1864, the day that the Democratic National Convention was to open in Chicago. It never took place because Northern spies and Confederate informers revealed the plan to Union authorities, and the Sons of Liberty failed

to keep their promises of support. Undaunted, Confederate secret agents planned raids on Northern prison camps and the burning of key Northern cities. Although several of these plots were carried out, none met with great success.

P

PICKETT, George Edward (1825–1875). This Confederate general is best remembered for the courageous but ill-fated assault on the Union lines that might have turned the Battle of Gettysburg into a Southern victory. Although he shared command with Generals James Johnston Pettigrew (1828–1863) and Isaac Ridgeway Trimble (1802–1888), the attack became known as Pickett's Charge. Pickett had graduated at the bottom of his West Point class in 1846. He then fought in the Mexican War and later in frontier campaigns against the Indians. A Virginian, he became a Southern general in 1862 and was badly wounded in the Seven Days' Battles in his home state. Pickett's Charge took place at Gettysburg on July 3, 1863. During the two previous days, General **Robert E. Lee** (*see*) had unsuccessfully struck the Union's left and right wings, firmly entrenched on two thickly wooded hills. On July 3, Lee ordered General **James Longstreet** (*see*) to launch a powerful frontal assault against the Union center on a low ridge nearly a mile from the Confederate lines. Longstreet delayed while the North strengthened its position, then finally ordered Pickett to form the brigades for the attack. After 150 Southern cannons had shelled the Union lines, 15,000 Confederate infantrymen started forward across open fields in perfect dress order

against the Northern center. A Union eyewitness saw "an overwhelming resistless tide of an ocean of armed men sweeping upon us . . . magnificent, grim, irresistible." Federal artillery tore into the Confederate ranks as they advanced. Only a handful of Southerners reached the Union line, and they were driven back after a brief, fierce struggle that marked the climax of the greatest battle of the war. Pickett returned to his lines with only 5,000 survivors. Trimble lost a leg in the charge and was captured, while Pettigrew, who survived the attack, was mortally wounded 10 days later. After Gettysburg, Pickett commanded in North Carolina and then led troops at Five Forks, Virginia, which was the rebel army's last assault of the war in the East. After the war, the Khedive of Egypt offered him a general's commission and later President **Ulysses S. Grant** (*see*) asked him to become a United States marshal. Pickett turned down both offers and became an insurance man in Virginia.

PICKETT'S CHARGE. *See* **Pickett, George.**

POPE, John (1822–1892). Unpopular with his troops, this Union general was defeated at the Second Battle of Bull Run in 1862 and was subsequently relieved of his command. A native of Kentucky, Pope graduated from West Point in 1842 and went on surveying expeditions in the West before fighting in the Mexican War. He returned to surveying duties after the war, and, when the Civil War started, he was made a brigadier general. After capturing Corinth, Mississippi, in October, 1862, Pope was given command of the newly established Army of

Virginia. Declaring that his headquarters would be "in the saddle," Pope antagonized his new troops in an address he made after taking command. Hinting that his soldiers lacked aggressiveness, he said, "Let us look before us and not behind. Success and glory are in the advance, disaster and shame lurk in the rear." Shortly thereafter, Pope's troops were routed at the Second Battle of Bull Run. Pope was subsequently relieved of command and spent the rest of the war in the West. Later in his career, he campaigned against the Sioux Indians.

PORTER, David Dixon (1813–1891). A Union naval hero, Porter went to sea at the age of 10 with his father, Commodore David Porter (1780–1843), who was engaged in suppressing piracy in the West Indies. He joined the Mexican navy as a midshipman in 1827, when Mexico was still fighting its war of independence with Spain. Porter returned to America two years later and then joined the American navy. He served in the Mediterranean, the South Atlantic, and the Gulf of Mexico. When the Civil War broke out, Porter, a native of Pennsylvania, was still only a lieutenant. He was promoted to the rank of commander in 1861. The following year, his mortar flotilla supported **David Farragut** (*see*), his fosterbrother, in the capture of New Orleans. Later that year, Porter, who had never even held the rank of captain or commodore, was promoted over 80 senior officers to acting rear admiral in command of the Mississippi squadron. He performed valuable service during the siege of Vicksburg and was promoted to rear admiral following its surrender on July 4, 1863. The following year, Porter was

given command of the North Atlantic Blockading Squadron with orders to attack Fort Fisher and other fortifications guarding the last Confederate stronghold at Wilmington, North Carolina. He captured the fort in 1865. Shortly after the war, Porter was appointed superintendent (1865–1869) of the United States Naval Academy. He was promoted to admiral of the navy after the death of Farragut in 1870. From 1877 until his own death, he was chairman of the Naval Board of Inspection.

PORTER, Fitz-John (1822–1901). This Union general spent more than 20 years trying to clear his

NATIONAL ARCHIVES

Fitz-John Porter

name after his court-martial in the Civil War. Early in the conflict, Porter, a West Point graduate (1845) and veteran of the Mexican War, was lauded for his leadership at the Seven Days' Battles in Virginia. At the Second Battle of Bull Run in August, 1862, he was ordered by General **John Pope** (*see*) to attack the right flank of the Confederate Army led

by **Stonewall Jackson** (*see*). The plan was to thus cut off Jackson from the troops of General **James Longstreet** (*see*). Porter failed to do so, and after the North's disastrous defeat, he was relieved of command and tried before a courtmartial. Pope accused Porter of disloyalty and failure to carry out an order. Porter declared that Longstreet's army had already joined Jackson's and that a successful attack would have been impossible. In spite of his defense, Porter was found guilty in 1863 and released from the army. He immediately began trying to clear his record, in the meantime working variously as a mining superintendent and merchant. In 1879, a board of generals reviewed his case and decided in his favor. Finally, on August 5, 1886, 23 years after his trial, Porter was reappointed to the army, as a colonel, without back pay. He retired from the service two days later. Before his death at the age of 79, Porter served as the commissioner of public works, police commissioner, and fire commissioner of New York City.

Q

QUANTRILL, William Clarke (1837–1865). Quantrill led a band of Confederate guerrillas known as Quantrill's Raiders that plundered communities in Kansas and Missouri during the Civil War. Born in Ohio, Quantrill went to Kansas in 1857. He tried farming but gave it up to teach school for a brief period, and then became a gambler, using the name Charley Hart. In 1860, Quantrill was charged with horse stealing in Lawrence, Kansas, and fled to avoid arrest. He then began kidnapping free blacks and selling them as slaves. Joining an anti-slavery group known as the Kansas Jayhawkers, he treacherously led them into an ambush laid by proslavery forces. When the Civil War began, Quantrill organized a band of marauders that included such outlaws as Jesse James (1847–1882). For several years, they pillaged pro-Union communities. Quantrill's most notorious raid, apparently carried out in revenge, took place on August 21, 1863, when his men burned the town of Lawrence, brutally murdering at least 150 persons. In May, 1865, near Louisville, Kentucky, Quantrill was shot and killed by a Union patrol.

R

RECONSTRUCTION ACTS.

The Reconstruction Acts, which consisted of one major act and three supplementary ones, were passed between 1867 and 1868. Although they were all vetoed by President **Andrew Johnson** (*see*), who advocated a mild policy toward the South, Congress, dominated by Radical Republicans who had gained control of both houses in 1866, overrode the vetoes. The four acts forced the Southern states to accept readmission to the Union under conditions that assured the Radical Republicans complete political control of the South. The first Reconstruction Act, which was passed on March 2, 1867, divided the Southern states—except for Tennessee, which had been readmitted to the Union in July, 1866 —into five military districts. Each was commanded by a major general who had dictatorial powers. This act also stated that, in order to gain readmission to the Union, the seceded states had to frame

new constitutions that guaranteed black voting rights. They also had to ratify the **Fourteenth Amendment** (*see*), which granted citizenship to blacks and prevented former Confederate officials from holding state or federal offices unless pardoned by a two-thirds vote of Congress. However, rather than accept these conditions, Southern whites chose to remain under martial law and made no attempts to call state constitutional conventions. Congress then reacted by passing the first supplementary Reconstruction Act on March 23, 1867. It empowered the military commanders to control registration and voting and to enforce the drafting of constitutions. It also authorized them to change the registration lists so that most former Confederate officials were excluded. A second supplementary act, passed on July 19, 1867, further extended the powers of the commanders, giving them complete control of the civil administrations of their districts. However, Southern whites continued to resist by refusing to vote on the newly framed constitutions. This made ratification impossible because the new constitutions had to be approved by a majority of the registered voters. Accordingly, on March 11, 1868, Congress passed a fourth Reconstruction Act. It declared that only a majority of the votes actually cast was needed for ratification. By June, 1868, seven of the 10 remaining Confederate states had been readmitted to the Union, and the rest were readmitted by July, 1870. The Radical Republicans maintained control in the South until the late 1870s, establishing an efficient but corrupt political machine that was bitterly resented by Southern whites. After the Radicals lost control, the

South staunchly supported the Democratic Party until the 1940s.

ROSECRANS, William S. (1819–

1898). Despite his defeat at the Battle of Chickamauga in September, 1863, Rosecrans was rated as one of the best strategists in the Union Army. After graduating from West Point in 1842, he served in the army for 12 years, resigning in 1854 to become an engineer and an architect. Rosecrans rejoined the army at the start of the Civil War and as a brigadier general in July, 1861, won one of the first battles of the conflict at Rich Mountain, Virginia. The next year, as commander of the Army of the Mississippi, he drove the rebels out of Iuka and Corinth, Mississippi, after bitterly fought battles. "Old Rosy," as his soldiers called him, took command of the new Army of the Cumberland in November, 1862, and forced Confederate General **Braxton Bragg** (*see*) to retreat at the Battle of Murfreesboro in Tennessee. Rosecrans and Bragg then faced each other for six quiet months until June, 1863, when Rosecrans maneuvered the Southern troops into Georgia. Bragg turned to fight at Chickamauga. The bloody battle, which produced more than 35,000 casualties, resulted in defeat for Rosecrans and the loss of his command. He next headed the Department of the Missouri for about a year and then had to wait for his next orders until March, 1867, when he resigned from the army. Rosecrans served as minister to Mexico (1868–1869) and then moved to California, where he was sent to Congress for two terms (1881–1885). His last post in the service of the government was as register (1885–1893) of the United States Treasury.

S

SHERIDAN, Philip Henry (1831–1888). In early August, 1864, this aggressive Union general received personal instructions from General **Ulysses S. Grant** (*see*) to drive the Confederates out of the so-called granary of the South, the Shenandoah Valley of Virginia, and to devastate the countryside so that, as Sheridan put it, "Crows flying over it . . . will have to carry their own provender [supplies]." His success added a new note of destruction to the war that **William T. Sherman** (*see*) expanded upon in his later march through Georgia. The son of Irish immigrants, Sheridan graduated from West Point in 1853. He then served in the Southwest and fought Indians in the Pacific Northwest. A quartermaster officer when the war began, Sheridan was appointed a colonel in the cavalry in May, 1862. Grant was so impressed by Sheridan's fighting ability that he made him a major general and chose him to reorganize the cavalry of the Army of the Potomac in the spring of 1864. That August, Grant gave Sheridan command of the Union Army in the Shenandoah Valley and ordered him to wage total war. Six weeks of bitter fighting against Confederate guerrillas followed. Then, on October 19, Confederate General **Jubal A. Early** (*see*) attacked Sheridan's camp at Cedar Creek, Virginia, in Sheridan's absence. Sheridan's swift ride 15 miles from Winchester to rally his men turned near-defeat into overwhelming victory. By March, 1865, Sheridan had laid waste the valley. Then, in April, at Petersburg, Virginia, Sheridan's army joined Grant in forcing the Confederates to retreat to Appomattox, where **Robert E. Lee** (*see*) surrendered. When the **Reconstruction Acts** (*see*) of 1867 were passed, Sheridan was appointed military commander of Louisiana and Texas. However, President **Andrew Johnson** (*see*) removed him from office after six months because of his severe and repressive policies and sent him to fight Indians in Missouri. Sheridan succeeded Sherman as commander in chief of the army in 1884. Four years later, he became a four-star general and published his *Personal Memoirs*.

SHERMAN, William Tecumseh (1820–1891). In a campaign late in 1864 to cut the Confederacy in two and sever its supply lines, Sherman led 62,000 Union troops across the state of Georgia. His army left a path of destruction 60 miles wide, burning plantations, homes, and crops as it proceeded to the Atlantic coast virtually unopposed. Sherman's march through Georgia left bitterness in the South that exists even today. Sometimes called the first modern general, Sherman believed in attacking and destroying enemy sources of supply. "War is all hell," he said in explaining that his march through Georgia was a military necessity. Sherman was born in Ohio and graduated from West Point in 1840. He served in the Mexican War but resigned his commission in 1853. After unsuccessful ventures in banking and law, in 1859 he became superintendent of the Louisiana Seminary of Learning and Military Academy (now Louisiana State University). He developed a genuine affection for the South and her people, but when Louisiana seceded, he volunteered for the Union Army. He fought at the First Battle of Bull Run and then became second in command of the federal forces in Kentucky. Sherman was temporarily relieved when his nervous temperament and abruptness resulted in reports that he was mentally deranged. In April, 1862, fighting under General **Ulysses S. Grant** (*see*), Sherman fought heroically at the Battle of Shiloh. He continued to perform well under Grant's command, and in March, 1864, when Grant was made commander of all Union forces, he put Sherman in command of military forces in the Western theater of operations. In May, 1864, Sherman moved out of Chattanooga to march on Georgia. His brilliant maneuvers defeated Confederate Generals **Joseph E. Johnston** and **John B. Hood** (*see both*) and, by September, Atlanta was Sherman's. He then received permission to march to the sea, waging "total war" on Georgia. Sherman abandoned Atlanta on November 15, 1864, burning the city before he left. He ordered his army to live off the countryside and to destroy war supplies, public buildings, railroads, and manufacturing centers. Private homes were not to be destroyed, but this order proved impossible to enforce. Soldiers and stragglers who joined the army committed many acts of vandalism. Sherman arrived in Savannah in time to present the city to President **Abraham Lincoln** (*see*) as a Christmas gift. His own estimate of the damages his men inflicted was $100,000,000. Proceeding north through the Carolinas, Sherman accepted the surrender of Johnston's troops just outside of Durham, North Carolina, on April 18, 1865. Although later repudiated by Radical Republicans in Congress, the peace terms offered by Sherman were very liberal. After the war, he remained in the army and served as commander in chief for 14 years (1869–1883).

STANTON, Edwin McMasters (1814–1869). Stanton, who was a prominent Ohio-born lawyer, served as Attorney General (1860–1861) under President James Buchanan (1791–1868) and then as Secretary of War (1862–1868) during the administrations of **Abraham Lincoln** and **Andrew Johnson** (*see both*). After becoming a lawyer in 1836, Stanton practiced in Ohio, Pittsburgh, and Washington, D.C., before being appointed Attorney General. As Secretary of War during the Civil War, Stanton did away with corrupt methods of awarding government contracts, instituted military control of railroads and telegraphs where needed, and—to the best of his ability—supplied the Union generals with the troops and supplies they needed. Some historians believe—although no proof has ever been uncovered—that Stanton knew of the plot to kill Lincoln and could have prevented the assassination. After the Civil War, Stanton sided with the anti-Southern Radical Republicans and opposed President Johnson's mild policy toward the South. In August, 1867, Johnson defied the **Tenure of Office Act** (*see*) and dismissed Stanton from his cabinet, but the Senate restored him to office the following January. Johnson, as a result, was impeached. When the President was acquitted in 1868, Stanton resigned. He was appointed to the Supreme Court in December, 1869, but died before he could take his seat.

STEVENS, Thaddeus (1792–1868). This grim-faced foe of slavery dominated American politics for 20 years. Stevens' Vermont boyhood, spent in poverty, made him compassionate to the poor and suspicious of the rich. Trained to be a lawyer, he moved in 1816 to Pennsylvania, where he often defended, without fee, fugitive slaves. He entered public life in the Pennsylvania legislature (1833–1841) and later served two terms (1849–1853) in Congress. There he assailed slavery as "a curse, a shame, and a crime." Stevens left the Whig Party in 1853 because of its moderate stand on slavery. He helped found the new Republican Party in Pennsylvania in 1855 and returned to Congress as a Republican three years later, serving for 10 years (1859–1868). Stevens warned the South that if it left the Union, "our next United States will contain no foot of ground on which a slave can tread, no breath of air which a slave can breathe." Toward the end of the Civil War, "Old Thad" urged the extermination of the Confederates. This view was partly inspired by the destruction in 1863 of Stevens' ironworks near Chambersburg, Virginia, where, he charged, the rebels "took all my horses, mules, and harness, even the crippled horses." After the war, Stevens demanded a stern reconstruction policy and denounced the more lenient policies of Presidents **Abraham Lincoln** and **Andrew Johnson** (*see both*). Calling the Southern states a "conquered province," he pushed through Congress in 1867 the first of several **Reconstruction Acts** (*see*), which called for military rule in the South. In 1868, Stevens led the fight to impeach Johnson, but his health was failing and he took little part in Johnson's trial. Before his death, Stevens asked to be buried in a small Lancaster, Pennsylvania, cemetery that accepted blacks. The epitaph he prepared for his tombstone describes his feelings:

I repose in this quiet and secluded spot, not from any natural preference for solitude, but, finding other cemeteries limited by charter rules as to race, I have chosen this, that I might illustrate in my death the principles which I advocated through a long life—Equality of Man before his Creator.

STUART, James Ewell Brown ("Jeb") (1833–1864). This dashing Confederate cavalry officer—he sported a plume in his hat and was accompanied by a trooper playing a banjo—was called "the eyes of the army" by General **Robert E. Lee** (*see*). Jeb Stuart twice humiliated Union forces by "riding around McClellan"—totally encircling the sluggish army of General **George B. McClellan** (*see*) in hit-and-run harassing operations. A native of Virginia, Stuart graduated from West Point in 1854 and then saw action in the Kansas border wars. As an aide to Lee, he helped crush the raid led by John Brown (1800–1859) at Harpers Ferry, Virginia, in 1859. Entering the Confederate Army in May, 1861, Stuart was commissioned a brigadier general after the First Battle of Bull Run. The daring Stuart's first ring-around-McClellan was executed in June, 1862, on a scouting mission for Lee during the Peninsular campaign. Four months later, his cavalry duplicated the dramatic maneuver, capturing hundreds of horses. Stuart fought well at the Second Battle of Bull Run, Antietam, and Fredericksburg. At Chancellorsville in May, 1863, he temporarily commanded the Second Army Corps after Generals **Stonewall Jackson** and **A. P. Hill** (*see both*) were wounded. During the Battle of Gettysburg in July of that same year, Stuart was criticized for a delay in getting intelli-

VALENTINE MUSEUM: COOK COLLECTION

J. E. B. Stuart

gence reports to Lee. Some historians say that Stuart, who had gone off on a raiding party on his own, was responsible for Lee's defeat at Gettysburg. Stuart was shot on May 11, 1864, while trying to halt the advance of General **Philip Sheridan** (*see*) on Richmond. He died the next day.

T

TENURE OF OFFICE ACT.

This act limited the President's power by requiring him to get the consent of the Senate before he could dismiss Presidential appointees. It was pushed through Congress on March 2, 1867, by anti-Southern Radical Republicans over the veto of President **Andrew Johnson** (*see*). Violation of the act was explicitly designated as a misdemeanor. Johnson believed that the act was unconstitutional. In order to bring a test case before the Supreme Court, he dismissed Secretary of War **Edwin Stanton** (*see*), an appointee of **Abraham Lincoln** (*see*). When the Court refused to hear the case, the Senate denied the dismissal, and General **Ulysses S. Grant** (*see*), who had been appointed in Stanton's place, turned the office back to Stanton. Johnson then ap-

pointed General Lorenzo Thomas (1804–1875) to the position. Stanton, however, barricaded himself in his office, and Thomas was unable to take over. Radical Republicans claimed Johnson was guilty of a misdemeanor and subsequently instituted impeachment proceedings. Much of the act was repealed in 1887, and in 1926 its principles were declared unconstitutional by the Supreme Court.

THIRTEENTH AMENDMENT.

The Thirteenth Amendment, which was ratified by the states on December 18, 1865, abolished slavery in the United States. It declared that "neither slavery nor involuntary servitude except as a punishment for crime whereof the party shall have been duly convicted, shall exist within the United States, or any place subject to their jurisdiction." It also gave Congress the power to enact laws to enforce abolition. The amendment thus constitutionally reinforced the **Emancipation Proclamation** (*see*) of 1863, which was a war measure that freed the slaves in Confederate-controlled areas. The proclamation did not affect slavery in border states that had remained loyal to the Union— Kansas, Maryland, and Missouri, for example. The Thirteenth Amendment was enacted in response to the post-Civil War need for a legal measure that would permanently abolish the institution of slavery.

THOMAS, George Henry (1816–1870).

A Virginia-born army officer who remained loyal to the Union during the Civil War, Thomas rallied federal troops at the Battle of Chickamauga in September, 1863, and won the nickname Rock of Chickamauga for his firm stand. Thomas, a

graduate of West Point in 1840, fought (1840–1842) against the Seminole Indians and in the Mexican War. He taught (1851–1854) at West Point and later served in Texas. In August, 1861, he was commissioned a brigadier general of volunteers in the Union Army and was given command of a division of the Army of the Ohio. On January 19, 1862, Thomas won the Battle of Mill Springs, Kentucky, which was the first Union victory in the West, thus forcing the Confederate Army out of eastern Kentucky. He was made a major general of volunteers the following April and was subsequently given command of one of the three corps that comprised the Army of the Cumberland under General **William S. Rosecrans** (*see*). His corps took part in the campaigns against Confederate General **Braxton Bragg** (*see*) in Tennessee. At the Battle of Chickamauga on September 19–20, 1863, Thomas managed to keep his troops in the field when most of Rosecrans' army fled. For this he was made brigadier general in the regular army the following October and subsequently replaced Rosecrans as commander of the Army of the Cumberland. In November, 1863, during the Chattanooga campaign, Thomas' army delivered two decisive blows against Bragg's forces at Lookout Mountain on November 24 and at Missionary Ridge the next day. Thomas' troops later played a major role in the Atlanta campaign of General **William T. Sherman** (*see*) in the summer of 1864. Thomas then returned to Tennessee, where he defeated General **John Bell Hood** (*see*) at Nashville on December 15–16, 1864, in one of the most clear-cut Union victories of the war. Promoted to major general, Thomas commanded the Tennessee region for the rest of the war. He remained in the army afterward and at the time of his death was commander of the Military Division of the Pacific.

TILDEN, Samuel J. (1814–1886). Tilden got the most popular votes for President in 1876 but lost the election by one vote in the electoral college. With 185 electoral votes needed for election, Tilden, a Democrat, got 184 and his opponent, Republican **Rutherford B. Hayes** (*see*) received 165. The 19 electoral votes of Florida, Louisiana, and South Carolina were in dispute, as well as one in Oregon. After much political maneuvering by both parties, an electoral commission made up of seven Republicans, seven Democrats, and one neutral was set up to decide the election. The "neutral"—Supreme Court Justice **Joseph P. Bradley** (*see*), who was a Republican—cast the deciding vote, and all the disputed votes were awarded to Hayes. A lawyer by profession, Tilden had entered politics in New York and, as Democratic state party chairman (1866–1874), he won a reputation as a political reformer by ousting the corrupt Tweed Ring from its stronghold in New York City. Tilden was elected governor of New York in

Samuel J. Tilden

1874 and continued his fight for reform by crushing the Canal Ring, a group of corrupt politicians who controlled the large sums of money used to maintain the state's canal system. After his loss to Hayes in 1876, Tilden retired from public life. He always maintained that he had been robbed of the Presidency. Many modern historians agree with his view.

TRENT AFFAIR. The *Trent* Affair was a diplomatic misunderstanding during the Civil War that almost resulted in war between Great Britain and the federal government. On November 7, 1861, at Havana, Cuba, James M. Mason (1798–1871) and John Slidell (1793–1871), two newly appointed Confederate ministers to Britain and France, respectively, boarded the British vessel *Trent*, which was bound for Europe. The following day, without instruction, Captain Charles Wilkes (1798–1877) of the Union vessel *San Jacinto* stopped and searched the *Trent* in the Bahama Channel. He arrested and removed the two Confederate statesmen and their secretaries and then took them to Boston, where they were all imprisoned. Wilkes had violated the American principle of freedom of the seas by searching a neutral vessel at sea and by seizing passengers from it, without bringing the ship and its passengers to port for an admiralty trial. Nevertheless, his action was widely acclaimed in the North. In Britain, however, it provoked anger and war fever. In a note delivered to Union authorities on December 23, 1861, the British government demanded an apology and the release of the prisoners within seven days. In the meantime, Britain sent 8,000 troops to Canada and

temporarily prohibited the exportation of war materials to the Union. War was averted when the federal government promised on December 26 to release the prisoners. Mason and Slidell were freed the following month and resumed their trip to Europe.

V

VALLANDIGHAM, Clement (1820–1871). Vallandigham was opposed to the Civil War and throughout it urged resistance to the draft and an end to the fighting. Born in Ohio, Vallandigham, a lawyer, was elected to the first of three terms in the House of Representatives in 1856. When the war began, Vallandigham helped to organize the Peace Democrats, who urged immediate negotiations. He called President **Abraham Lincoln** (*see*) "King" Lincoln and accused him of destroying the Constitution. In 1863, Vallandigham was arrested and charged with treasonous activities. When a military court sentenced him to prison, Vallandigham protested that the army had no right to try him. Lincoln intervened and commuted his sentence to banishment to the Confederacy. Vallandigham went to the South but after a while decided to live in exile in Canada. While there, he ran unsuccessfully for governor of Ohio in 1863 and was made supreme commander of the Sons of Liberty, a secret pro-Southern organization. He accepted funds from the Confederacy to finance an unsuccessful uprising in the Midwest known as the **Northwest Conspiracy** (*see*). In June, 1864, Vallandigham sneaked over the Canadian border and began campaigning for a peace plank in the Democratic platform. The plank

LIBRARY OF CONGRESS

was inserted, but the Democratic candidate, **George B. McClellan** (*see*), refused to support it. After the war, Vallandigham labored to restore the Democratic Party to its former prominence. He died while defending an accused murderer. To prove in court that the slain man had in actuality shot himself, Vallandigham pointed a pistol at his head and shot himself. His client was subsequently acquitted.

W

WADE, Benjamin Franklin (1800–1878). A Senator (1851–1869) from Ohio, Wade was the chairman of the Joint Committee on the Conduct of the War, which sought to gain Congressional control of the conduct of the Civil War. The committee was set up shortly after the outbreak of the Civil War by Wade and other anti-Southern Radical Republicans to demand decisive military action. It worked closely with Secretary of War **Edwin Stanton** (*see*) and constantly criticized the way President **Abraham Lincoln** (*see*) directed the war. Wade, a native of Massachusetts, moved to Ohio as a young man and eventually, after working as a farmer, laborer, and teacher, became a lawyer in 1828. He was first elected to the state senate in 1837 and soon became known for his strong antislavery views. He quickly assumed leadership of radical abolitionists in Congress upon his election to the Senate in 1851. In 1864, when Lincoln vetoed a harsh reconstruction plan that Wade had helped to formulate, Wade issued his most bitter condemnation of Lincoln's war and reconstruction policies. However, pressure from his constituents forced him to support Lincoln in the final weeks of the 1864 election. When Vice-President **Andrew Johnson** (*see*) became President upon Lincoln's death and voiced approval of his predecessor's humane reconstruction policies, Wade became one of the leaders of the effort to impeach him. In 1867, Wade was elected president pro tempore of the Senate, to preside over that body in the absence of a Vice-President. Had Johnson been convicted at his impeachment trial, Wade would have become President.

WALKE, Henry (1808–1896). A Union naval officer born and raised in Virginia, Walke commanded gunboats that aided in several Northern victories in the Civil War. Walke entered the navy in 1827 and saw action in the Mexican War. At the outset of the Civil War, he commanded a supply ship at Pensacola, Florida, and, when the navy yard there was seized by the South in January, 1861, he entered it under a truce flag and led its garrison and noncombatants to New York. Although he was subsequently court-martialed and convicted for leaving his station to rescue the garrison, Walke was only lightly admonished. He then joined the flotilla commanded by **Andrew Foote** (*see*) on the upper Mississippi River. As captain of the gunboat *Carondelet* in February, 1862, Walke played an important role in the capture of Fort Donelson, Tennessee, and later raced past the batteries at Island No. 10 in the Mississippi—an action that has been called "one of the most daring and dramatic events of the war." Promoted to captain in July, 1862, Walke commanded the ironclad *Lafayette* in the Vicksburg campaign and later pursued Confederate raiders in the Atlantic aboard the *Sacramento*. Although he was eventually promoted to rear admiral after the war, he felt slighted by his assignments and retired in 1871. Complaining to President **Ulysses S. Grant** (*see*), Walke asserted that he had "fought more for his country than any other officer in the navy" during the Civil War.

WHEELER, Joseph (1836–1906). One of the youngest Confederates to hold an important command, Wheeler was only 26 when he was appointed a brigadier general in 1862. He had graduated from West Point in 1859, but he resigned from the federal army at the outbreak of the Civil War two years later and was appointed colonel of the 19th Alabama Infantry. After fighting at the Battle of Shiloh in April, 1862, Wheeler was put in command of the cavalry of the Army of the Mississippi in July, 1862. Nicknamed Fightin' Joe, Wheeler and his cavalry took part in nearly 200 battles and 800 skirmishes, during which he was wounded three times and had 16 horses shot out from under him. He accompanied the advance of General **Braxton Bragg** (*see*) into Kentucky in the early fall of

Joseph Wheeler

NATIONAL ARCHIVES

1862 and participated in the subsequent Murfreesboro and Chickamauga campaigns in the winter of 1862–1863. During one daring raid against the federal army in October, 1863, Wheeler's men destroyed more than 1,200 Union wagons. After taking part in the siege of Knoxville a month later, his cavalry harassed the troops of General **William T. Sherman** (*see*) during their march from Atlanta to the sea in November–December, 1864. After the war, Wheeler settled in Alabama, where he became a planter and lawyer. A tireless advocate of reconciliation between the North and the South, Wheeler served briefly in the House of Representatives in 1881–1882 and again in 1883 and then was elected to eight consecutive terms (1885–1900). During the Spanish-American War, he served as a major general of volunteers. Again in command of cavalry, he helped defeat the Spanish at Las Guasimas, Cuba, on June 24, 1898, and was present a week later at the Battle of San Juan Hill on July 1. From 1899 to 1900, Wheeler briefly commanded a brigade in the Philippines before finally retiring as a brigadier general of the regular army.

WHISKEY RING. This name has been given to a conspiracy that operated from about 1867 until 1875. Its leading members were whiskey distillers, mainly from St. Louis, Milwaukee, and Chicago, and officials of the Internal Revenue Service and other government agencies. The distillers bribed the officials in order to keep for themselves the federal taxes on distilled whiskey, which at that time were extremely high. They ultimately defrauded the government of more than $3,000,000. When the ring's activities were uncovered during the second administration of **Ulysses S. Grant** (*see*), 238 persons—including Grant's private secretary **Orville E. Babcock** (*see*)—were indicted by federal grand juries, and 110 of them were convicted. The scandal led many persons to believe that the ring had been raising money for the Republican Party and that Grant himself had been involved. In the Presidential campaign of 1876, the main issues were government corruption and reform, and both the Republican candidate, **Rutherford B. Hayes,** and his Democratic opponent, **Samuel Tilden** (*see both*), were nominated on the basis of their honest reputations.

WINSLOW, John Ancrum (1811–1873). A Union naval officer, Winslow carried out one of the most celebrated naval engagements of the Civil War when his warship, the *Kearsarge,* sank the famed Confederate raider *Alabama* off Cherbourg, France, on September 19, 1864 (*see p. 693*). The United States government later filed claims against the British for the damage that the *Alabama,* a raider built in Britain, had caused. This dispute was not settled until 1873. Born in North Carolina, Winslow entered the United States Navy as a midshipman at the age of 16, fought in the Mexican War, and was made a commander in 1855. After the outbreak of the Civil War, Winslow served on the Mississippi River flotilla and was promoted to captain in 1862. From 1863 to 1864, he was skipper of the *Kearsarge,* which was on the lookout for Confederate vessels in European waters. Winslow was hailed as a hero and made a commodore for sinking the *Alabama,* which was captained by Raphael Semmes (1809–1877). For the remainder of the war, Winslow promoted the Union cause at civic celebrations throughout the North. He later commanded the Gulf squadron (1866–1867), and, after being appointed rear admiral in 1870, he took charge of the Pacific fleet for two years.

WOOD, Fernando (1812–1881). As the mayor of New York City in January, 1861, Wood, a wealthy merchant and Democratic leader, proposed that New York secede from the Union. Wood had been a leader of New York City's Tammany Hall, but he alienated other Democratic leaders and formed his own organization, known as the Mozart Hall faction, after the building where it met. Wood was elected mayor of New York three times (1854–1857 and 1859–1861). He had many Southern friends and led a pro-Southern delegation to the Democratic National Convention in 1860. Two years later, he was elected to the House of Representatives. A vigorous opponent of the war, Wood, together with **Clement Vallandigham** (*see*) and others, organized the Peace Democratic Party in 1863. They favored peace by negotiation and were accused of having Confederate sympathies. They were often called Copperheads, after the snake that strikes without warning. They turned the insult into a symbol of their cause by wearing Indian-head copper pennies as badges. Wood's brother, Benjamin Wood (1820–1900), owned the original New York *Daily News* and supported his brother's Copperhead position. When **Abraham Lincoln** (*see*) was reelected in 1864, Wood was defeated for his House seat, but he returned to Congress in 1867 and served in the House until his death.